The Ultimate Guide to His Point of View

Most guys' ability to fantasize has been honed to a razor edge, and we spend far more time than you can possibly imagine picturing women in various states of undress. But contrary to popular opinion, all men are not pigs. (Except when we're with our friends, and you're not supposed to be there anyway!) In fact, what we look for in women is far from the stereotypical image.

from *What Men Want From the Women They Love*

What Men Want

From The Women They Love

KEN CARLTON

COSMOPOLITAN®

WHAT MEN WANT FROM THE WOMEN THEY LOVE is an original publication of Cosmopolitan Books. This work has never before appeared in book form.

The purpose of this book is to educate and entertain. It is sold with the understanding that the publisher and author are not rendering medical, psychological, or other professional services. The publisher and author shall not be liable or responsible to any person or entity with respect to any loss or damage caused or alleged to be caused directly or indirectly by the information that appears in this book.

COSMOPOLITAN BOOKS
AVON BOOKS
A division of
The Hearst Corporation
1350 Avenue of the Americas
New York, New York 10019

Copyright © 1994 by Ken Carlton
Published by arrangement with the author
Library of Congress Catalog Card Number: 94-94321
ISBN: 0-380-77497-6

First Cosmopolitan Books Printing: February 1996

COSMOPOLITAN TRADEMARK REG. U.S. PAT. OFF. AND IN OTHER COUNTRIES, MARCA REGISTRADA, HECHO EN U.S.A.

Printed in the U.S.A.

RA   10   9   8   7   6   5   4   3   2   1

Acknowledgments

My thanks to Judith Newman, who recognized that our many years of gossiping on the phone could well translate into a book like this. To Marjorie Braman, who went to bat for me from day one and gave me the opportunity to speak out on behalf of the entire male gender. My special gratitude to Nancy Kalish for her meticulous attention to detail, as well as her wise advice that will no doubt put all of these revelations in a fair and positive light. To Blossom, for helping me survive the crisis of the lost disk. And my special thanks to Katherine Tasheff, not only for her valuable assistance, but also for showing me how a "single" guy can become a happy boyfriend. Her input was integral to the perspective of this book.

KRC

Contents

Part Two
THE LONG RUN

Introduction

When word got around that I was writing a book entitled *What Men Want From the Women They Love*, I was most amused by the varied reactions of my friends. John, an old college buddy who had been privy to a dozen years of my dating escapades, insisted that if I wrote a true expose, I'd have to turn in my "Man Card." He was of the school of thought that most men's secrets are best kept in the locker room. I heard via the grapevine that several of my former (and short-lived) girlfriends asked: "What the heck does *he* know about what men want? When he was dating me he had no clue what he wanted!" But I think my friend, Julia, captured the spirit of the project best. She said the book should be called <u>Beyond</u> *Great Sex and Big Breasts: What <u>ELSE</u> Men Want From the Women They Love.*

I got the message loud and clear. The average, single, dating male has long been saddled with the unfair stereotype that "all men are pigs." My mission was to prove that all men are *not!* We do date and we do get involved. We have hearts and feelings and a tremendous desire to be struck in love and settle down with the woman of our dreams.

If you believe that timing is everything, then perhaps I have tackled this book at exactly the right moment in my life. I've dated enough to know what makes for a great and promising romance . . . and what portends an awkward and meaningless affair. I have been involved in several lengthy relationships that have teetered on the brink of marriage, yet I have been fortunate enough to see them end, appropriately, before two mismatched people found themselves walking down the aisle. Today I am riding the wave of an exciting relationship and have gained infinite wisdom on the subject of commitment.

Beyond that, I bring another important perspective to this book. While I consider myself "one of the guys," I still have a wealth of incredibly close "friend-girls." The men you are going to meet are my buddies, and friends of friends, and men of all ages and professions who *wanted to talk*. These are real guys with real stories, definitely not edited to soothe or impress. Some of the tales are a bit rough around the edges, yet many are sincerely touching. In either case they are true and from the heart, and hopefully, rather revealing. Still, I don't think the picture would be complete without including the many conversations I had with women. Some of my most poignant insights came from listening to "the other half of the story."

This book is about breaking down the barrier between the sexes. Large sections of what you read will fall under the category of male confessional. In this age of the "politically correct," it is not always easy for men to come clean. Some of the stereotypes are true. For example, we *do* think about sex, on the average, every forty-five seconds. I have spared no details on the male psyche. While some of what you read may seem unusual, even shocking, it is never intended to dictate a norm or suggest an expectation.

While sex often looms large in male discussions, I've also gone to great lengths to delve deeply into the many other subjects that men talk about with their guy friends—career concerns, children, fear of commitment, the responsibility of married life—in order to portray the kinds of traits we are looking for in a serious girlfriend.

For all the talk though, the most essential, yet intangible element of every successful relationship is chemistry, and that is the one thing we all have to leave up to fate. This book cannot define the nature of "the spark" between two people, nor will it answer for the behavior of the entire male gender. But having spoken to hundreds of men and women, I know firsthand that we are all in this game for the same reason. We want to wake up together on a Sunday morning and weigh such monumental life choices as: Who gets out of bed to make the coffee? Do we want to make love, or throw on our jeans and slip out for a movie? Are we content enough as a couple to spend the whole day reading the paper, and napping away the time wrapped happily in each others' arms?

This book will uncover some of the most honest revelations about men you would ever want to know. And hopefully it will provide answers to some questions you were dying to ask. I extend my thanks to the couples and the single men and women who were brave and willing enough to pour their hearts out to me. I believe they did it for the very reason I have written this book—to open the door for honest communication between the sexes, and improve all of our chances for finding an exciting and satisfying relationship.

KRC
July 12, 1994—New York City

PART ONE

BOYS JUST WANT TO HAVE FUN

CHAPTER 1:

The Chase

Rob, a 27-year-old New Yorker, seemingly had it all. He boasted good looks, an engaging personality, and a high-paying job at a prestigious investment bank. Combine these traits with a passion for sailing, ease on the tennis court, and an encyclopedic knowledge of French films, and you'd assume that his personal calendar was overflowing. However, this was not the case. Despite his easygoing charm and a twenty-sixth-floor luxury apartment in Manhattan, Rob was having one hell of a time finding a girlfriend. Reluctant to resort to the Personals, or one more setup from his concerned mother, he was just about ready to resign himself to a life of long work hours and solo bagels with his Sunday *Times* when he experienced that intangible "click," that floored-by-love-at-first-sight feeling. It struck at the most unexpected moment.

While gulping his morning coffee and flipping through the morning news shows, he came upon a segment featuring ten college women being honored in New York for their academic achievements.

3

He let the remote control rest while each woman introduced herself to the enthusiastic morning host.

Rob's "click" came when the fifth honoree had her fifteen seconds of fame. Fresh out of college and about to begin her first job as an editorial assistant, Suzanne recited a few forgettable facts to the morning anchor, and Rob was entranced.

He was also in luck. One of his best friends was a producer at the network where Suzanne had just appeared. A quick phone call netted him the necessary info. The ten women were to be wined and dined at a glitzy Manhattan nightclub that evening, and a select group of young men were being recruited as escorts. Rob's friend arranged for him to be one of them.

That evening, Suzanne and Rob met. They had dinner together. They danced. They got along okay. Then Suzanne shook Rob's hand and went back home to her boyfriend in Brooklyn. Some fairy tale romance, right? Well, the story wasn't over yet.

Not one to be put off by something as insignificant as a "significant other," Rob stayed in touch with Suzanne. He bought her dinner now and then, sent flowers on her birthday, spirited her away for occasional bike rides in the park, and even offered her a shoulder to cry on when her young (and artsy) boyfriend decided he needed some "space."

Fortunately for Rob, the space was in eastern Europe. Budapest, to be exact. Even the phones were conveniently inconvenient. And so, Rob made his move, switching from low-key friendship to a nine-month courtship that he pursued with every ounce of energy he had previously put into his high-flying career. The former boyfriend was gently disposed of by a long-distance letter. Rob and Suzanne were married a year later, and today they are happily raising their two children.

Have you sat at home one Saturday night too many? Are you thoroughly disenchanted with yet another "Girls Night Out" devoted to discussing what's wrong with the entire male gender? The fact is, we men have also spent one too many nights out with "the boys." Life is not like the beer commercial, where men turn to each other and say, "Why ask why?" And we all aren't waiting for our future mates to miraculously appear on a TV show we happen to be watching.

We *do* ask women out. Many women! And sometimes women ask us out. And throughout this whole dating process, we get interested, we get horny, we get involved, we get rejected, we get revenge and sometimes, believe it or not, we get serious. But before all this fun can begin, something *you* do has to get us attracted (which, in turn, compels us to get your phone number).

The Hook

Try as we may, there is no hiding from the advertising and media assault that tells men that all women should have flowing hair, sparkling teeth, and perfect breasts. Of course, the same source also tells women that we men are supposed to boast great butts, adorable smirks, and thick heads of hair. Ahhh, if only the world were so perfect.

In reality, what men look for in a date is far from the stereotypical image. As a matter of fact, most men are really seeking imperfections. Cute, quirky, off-the-wall aspects of your personality and looks that make you stand out from the crowd, or more specifically, from our last awful date (the one who made us swear off dating for the rest of our lives)!

Let's start with first appearances. We all do. (Be honest. How many times have you called a friend to talk about a guy you just met, and told her, "He's butt ugly, but what a stellar personality!") We have to be attracted to something about you, so unless your last name is Rockefeller, looks count— but not the way most women assume they do.

Perhaps large breasts, more than any other feature, are symbolic of everything women do not understand about men. Granted, we will walk into oncoming traffic to see a "nice pair," but they do not have to be large. Those that are simply unencumbered, untethered, or aroused will do the trick. When we are shamelessly gawking, it is not the size of the breasts that necessarily intrigues us, but the accessibility. The same applies to legs and butts. Everyone's got them. But the ones on display are the ones that attract the most attention. This is not a call for all women to start dressing like hookers on a sultry August night. It is just an admission that biologically, when flesh is on display, we must look.

This is good news, because it means there is no specific image you have to live up to. There are men drawn to pendulous breasts, and those who lose control at a mere blip on the bra chart. And for every man who has a rear-end collision in traffic from gazing at a long-haired blonde, there are a dozen guys who will date only bobbed brunettes. Front teeth with spaces between them, knobby knees, unshaven armpits—the number of unpredictable features the male species finds attractive can hardly be counted. The point is, it isn't necessarily how you look but how you *wear* your looks. If you are not a certain man's type, all the preparation in the world isn't going to change that. On the other hand, *whatever* your particular look might be, if you wear it with the confidence of a woman who is comfortable and happy with herself, whether you realize it or not, every day on a street corner or in an elevator some guy will see you and run back to his office clutching his heart because he is sure you're the woman of his dreams and he doesn't know how to get your phone number.

Most guys' ability to fantasize has been honed to a razor edge, and we spend far more time than you can possibly imagine picturing you in various states of undress. Yet, despite the less-than-complimentary maxim, "All men are pigs," all men are NOT. (Except when we're with our friends, and you're not supposed to be there anyway!) Many single men are nice guys with a void in their personal lives, looking for someone to bring home to Mom. And they'll generally rule out the silly-looking bombshell in the peek-a-boo dress as too ridiculous to be seen with.

If we are chatting you up at a party, then we've already imagined you naked and liked what we saw. Should we ever get that far, we will be happy campers. In the meantime, we'll be checking out your personality, and to most men, personality is everything. We are far less harsh about looks than you might think, but far tougher on personality than you realize.

A man is looking for a woman he can communi-

cate with, someone with whom he shares some
common interests. Food, movies, art—these are all
jumping-off points to a first, second, third date,
and more. Sports can be the ultimate litmus test for
many a potential couple. If you've got your eye on
a workmate who is buried in the sports pages every morning, and you enjoy a day at the ballpark
yourself, use this to your advantage. Drop a few
stats, moan about the home team's lack of pitching. Then watch the man's eyes light up. It's a
golden opportunity for a guy to take the hint and
ask you out.

On the other hand, if you'd rather have root canal work than spend sixty seconds watching a
sporting event, don't try to fake it. Trying to mold
your personality to a man's ideal is about as comfortable as wearing high heels a size and a half too
small, and the result will probably be about as
pleasant. Sure, you might be able to tolerate a few
innings of baseball for the sake of a hot date, but
long after the bracing first kisses have faded, a
man who loves sports will still be glued to ESPN,
while you're fretting to your girlfriends on the
phone in the next room.

Don't be bashful about your extracurricular activities. Hunting for a soulmate bears a lot of re-
semblance to searching for a job, and any man who
has been on enough dates knows how to read the
resume. Fred, an avid skier and outdoorsman, will
not date a woman who raves about Florida, St.
Thomas, or Club Med. Not that there is anything
wrong with a good beach vacation, but he has
learned that women who swoon at the mention of
a tropical island probably won't buy into his ultimate dream life of chopping wood in Montana. In

those precious first meetings, we have little to cling to beyond your mysterious smile and the stories you tell. Granted, in the final tally, we long to be so compatible that we do nothing but lie in bed and snooze away the weekend together. But unless we are an incredibly forward couple, we're probably going to have to go on a few dates before that can happen.

So, you graduated Stanford Phi Beta Kappa at the age of sixteen. You've jumped out of planes, fed starving children in Somalia, and you can whip up a bouillabaisse with the best French chefs. Yet while every other woman at your office is out on a merry-go-round of dates, your longest relationship in the past five years has been with the checkout kid at the video store. Why is it that there are so many women with everything going for them who can't seem to land one good date? Perhaps the answer lies in confidence, both your own and the confidence you instill in the man who is fawning over you.

Take a party, for instance. We all suffer indescribable terror at the thought of baring our souls at a gathering that essentially has "meat market" written all over it. Still, parties are a necessary evil. Look around you at the next major get-together of single people. If one has to generalize, the women will all look terrific, well-dressed, and nicely put together. The men will all be practiced slobs, uniformly wearing ripped Levi's and slightly rumpled dress shirts.

Now picture the mental preparation for this event. You have spent time and money and given some degree of thought as to how you will appear in the crowd. You look like you are ready for action. But a man's attitude is, "Heck, we'll stop by the party, check it out, and if it sucks, we can always split and go knock back beers somewhere else!" This is how we cover up our lack of confidence. We downplay the event, and essentially make a non-appearance.

Inevitably, men notice that the women who appear to be having the best time at a party are the ones who also seem to not give a damn. Somehow, this makes them seem more accessible for conversation or flirtation. We're much more likely to approach a woman who looks relaxed about the whole affair; someone in jeans and a tee with a great smile who shares the same disdain we have for meeting at a party. The stunning six-foot knockout made up like a doll and dressed to the nines is intimidating. Some of us might work up the nerve to line up for her number or otherwise come on to her if we get the chance. But it's likely that rejection will soon follow, and we'll skulk away from a pouty-faced model type, dragging our crushed ego behind us.

On the other hand, when a couple of fellas who are holding up the keg see a couple of easygoing gals having a laugh in the corner, we are more prone to saunter over and invest a few of our carefully crafted quips. For example: "Party stinks, huh? Wanna get outta here?" Or the old classic, "My friend dragged me here. Don't you just hate these things?"

Men suffer confidence crises just like you. Harry, a Boston-based writer, spent six months flirting with a New York advertising executive, waiting for a signal, any signal, before he asked her out. It wasn't that he couldn't ask her out. It's just that he wanted some kind of a sign, a tip-off, that he wasn't about to make a complete buffoon out of himself. Granted, there is a class of male, usually found at construction sites, who makes his stance rather clear, wanted or not. But in the daily course of life, there are plenty of men who need a little nudge. Try us. Say, "Nice tie, Bill. You always wear the neatest ties," and Bill thinks, "Gee, she notices my ties. What else does she notice?" He puts two and two together, and the rest, as they say, is history.

The First Date

Science may never adequately explain how chemistry between two people actually works. Yet, we all know how it feels. When our glance is returned by a stranger at a party or during a lingering conversation at the office coffee machine, something clicks. We may have been out of sync with the last hundred people we met, but now our hormones are raging. Our faces are flushed crimson and we're dreaming of growing old on a porch in Vermont with this person we don't even know. It is an indescribable emotion, an affirmation of everything we know about ourselves, an essence that could almost be bottled, it's so strong. One problem, though. We still operate within the social convention of dating, and no matter how powerful the chemistry between two people may be, one of us still has to work up the nerve to ask the other one out. Some of us are better at this than others.

Brian, a Washington, D.C. businessman, known to his friends as "The Dating King," had a legendary modus operandi. He was the founder (and one

of the most successful practitioners) of the triple-
header: Three successive dates with three different
women in one evening. Date one was exploratory,
almost always a first date for cocktails after work.
This gave him a safe venue to check out a new interest. Date two was dinner, usually with a woman
he deemed to have potential (probably from a re-
cent cocktail date), and it ran from, say, eight to
eleven. Brian's dinner dates were always professional women because they generally needed to be
home by midnight. Date three was reserved for
artist-types with a penchant for staying out late. As
Brian so aptly put it, "They were the most likely to
go to bed with me on a weeknight." Talk about
covering your bases.

Although not all men are as precise in their intentions, there actually is some rhyme and reason
to the various invitations we serve up for a first or
second date. The drinks-after-work scene is a safe
scenario that men like to practice on blind or risky
dates. If conversation is scintillating and interest
blooms, we can quickly segue into dinner together.
But if the date has zero potential written all over it,
what better way to slip out of an awkward situation than to excuse ourselves gracefully after one
boring beer?

The weeknight dinner date straddles the line between a business get-together and something a tad
more personal. We are both already dressed for
work, so there's no worry about how to look.
We've been busy at our jobs all day, so conversation should be plentiful. And if it goes well, we can
either stay out really late or plan ahead for the next
date, before our first one comes to an end.

When it comes to making weekend plans, you

can glean a lot based on which night we ask you
out for. The Friday night date suggests a hint of
craziness. For some reason, men's hormones rage
on Friday nights. We want to drink heavily, play
poker, or have sex. (Or all three, if it's a really good
evening.) So, if a man asks you out for a Friday
night, odds are he is not thinking about a quiet romantic interlude at a moody cafe. A sporting event
or the neighborhood pub will probably be on the
agenda.

Saturday night is "Date Night," and everyone in
the world knows this. In New York, Paris, Hong
Kong, and Wichita, Kansas, if you ask someone out
for a date on Saturday, you mean business. Now
don't be put off by this. Accepting does not mean
you are ready to get married. But guys ask women
out for a Saturday night because there is something romantic about it. Saturday night is fraught
with passion and mystery and the implied suggestion that it might just end well into Sunday morning. More first sexual encounters probably take
place in the wee hours of Saturday than on any
other night of the week.

And then there's Sunday. Sunday! The most creative day of the week for the bold and adventurous. Just picture the possibilities. First of all, there's
Sunday brunch. Beware of turning this invite
down if you are fond of a man, for he will immediately assume that: (a) you refused him because
you are sleeping with someone else, or (b) you refused him because you have a Saturday night date
and *might* be sleeping with someone else by Sunday morning. On the other hand, when you say
yes to Sunday brunch, it opens his mind to all sorts
of marvelous images. He pictures you waking up

alone in your college nightshirt, reading your
newspaper, legs tucked underneath you on your
favorite chair, sipping coffee, noshing on a bagel,
all those trivial worries of the week left far, far behind. And somehow you always look more re-
freshed and wonderful when you meet him on a
Sunday wearing fun, weekend clothes with your
hair pulled back and a rosy glow to your freshly
showered cheeks. Perhaps men love the Sunday
brunch date because it gives us a hint of what our
everyday lives together might be like. Sunday is
full of romantic possibilities. A picnic in the park,
a trip to the zoo, or a midday stroll through the
city all carry the breezy implication that we can get
on well together for a lazy afternoon.

The logistics of the first few dates can also be a
tricky subject. When should you offer to pay and
for what? This is a politically charged question for
both parties. Men want to pay for everything because it makes us feel strong, successful, powerful,
and in control. These are all good reasons why a
woman should *want* to split the check. Why relin-
quish all that satisfaction to a man?

On the other hand, dating is expensive. Here's a
breakdown of an average date in New York City (if
you live in a city where people have cars, replace
cab costs with gas and parking): We pick you up
and take a cab to a downtown bar for drinks: $30.
Dinner at a normal Italian restaurant, nothing
fancy, but including appetizers, a bottle of wine,
dessert, and coffee: $80. After-dinner drinks (why
is Bailey's so expensive?): $10 for a couple of snif-
ters, easy. At this point we're either drunk, having
a great time, or both, and since neither of us wants
to call it an evening, we go out for jazz and a cou-

ple of beers: $50. Now it's 3:00 a.m. and the night is winding down. It's been three hours since dinner, so we stop for a slice of pizza and a soda, and the true gentleman in us sneaks out and buys you a dozen roses from the twenty-four hour corner store: $20.

That comes to almost two hundred hard-earned cash dollars for a casual date. No theater tickets, no rock concert, no ballet. Just drinks and dinner and a little jazz. Do we want you to help us pay? Absolutely not. Is it okay for you to chip in? Only for one round of drinks and one cab ride—although definitely not the last cab ride to your apartment. If you pick up the tab for that one and let us go without walking you to your door, then we will assume that you hated the evening, don't want a kiss good night, and consider our sexual potential right up there with a clammy handshake from your boss at the office Christmas party! So, yes, it's fine for you to lay out ten to twenty dollars on a date, as long as it is a thoughtful contribution, and *not* an insistent one. It is very off-putting to have a woman nearly break a man's arm insisting that she pay for something. However, he's apt to be genuinely touched when you offer to buy a round at the pub. It's just the right amount of generosity, plus it gives us the opportunity to say, "Thank you, no," if we so choose.

In this day of equal rights, other gender-role-bending questions arise: When should a woman do the asking out? How do men feel about the reversal of the traditional roles? And for that matter, why haven't women leapt at the opportunity to take the power position and initiate that first date? For all the women who say it is fair play and they *do* ask men out, almost any currently single man will tell you that he's been asked out on a date maybe once in his life.

Equality aside, the male ego is a very fragile thing, and a woman who asks a man out needs to operate under a slightly modified set of rules. Unless of course, she wants to "wear the pants" and really reverse the roles: do the asking, set the time, choose the evening's activity, *and* pick up the tab. That's a bold—and exciting—move. When a woman controls a date, is she going to take the sexual initiative too? Will you walk us to our door and work up the nerve to go for that first kiss? Will you wait for us to ask you in and then go through all the little moves *we've* been perfecting for years, trying to get us into bed? And if all that works out well, are you still in the driver's seat, while we wait by the phone hoping you'll call? The only real way to find out is to test the waters. The worst thing that can happen is you'll get rejected. We have, all our lives, and trust me: It is not the end of the world.

But there is a way you can ask a man out without stealing his thunder: the friendly, informal proposition. Suggesting drinks after work to a potential office paramour is incredibly safe—and very clear. If you really wanted to talk about that new computer program, you wouldn't have suggested doing it during "happy hour" on a Friday night. So your "work-related invite" sends a message, yet leaves us a safe out. We can beg off entirely, or go along and actually talk about work. On the other hand, if passions have been brewing, now you have gotten us out of the office, and with your encouragement, you've given us an opportunity to pursue you further, beyond the realm of anything that could be construed as sexual harassment in the workplace.

Another avenue of easy flirtation is the group date. This is a little nervier, because you are asking us out for a social occasion. But the situation still provides you with a decent safety zone because you are hiding your romantic curiosity behind a large gathering of people. The classic group date is the weekend barbecue. Lisa, an employee at a huge corporation, was invited to a softball party at a neighborhood park—a day of beer, burgers, and games. She chose this as the right time to find out if Tad, an associate at another firm, had been harmlessly flirting with her at several previous meetings, or if he harbored a real interest. She asked him if he played ball or drank beer (yes to both), and did he want to join her, and one hundred of her not-so-close friends at the park? Tad readily accepted. They spent a great casual day together, and they got to see each other in real clothes as opposed to business suits. When the softball game was over, they had the perfect opportunity to go out for dinner and spend the remainder of the evening getting to know each other even better. Four months later, they moved in together.

Lisa acted on a hunch she had about Tad. He might never have asked her out, because from a business standpoint it could have been seen as a conflict of interest. But Lisa took charge and cleared the way for a great relationship. If you ask a man to join you for a company picnic and he starts to list his allergies, take this as a no and move on. If you invite him to a group event and he brings six friends, including his girlfriend, consider this a negative as well. But if you sense a hint of interest from a man you get along with, and he just has been extremely slow in asking you out, take the plunge! Most guys would, at the very least, consider it very complimentary. And as weathered veterans of rejection, we have more than a little empathy. If we're truly not interested, we'll try to find a polite and inoffensive way to let you down.

Playing the Game

Now, how are we supposed to behave if we really enjoyed our first date with you? Should we call the next morning and say, "Gee Marge, that was a stupendous evening. Best time I've had since grammar school. I really think you're the greatest. We're just amazing together, aren't we???" This may be honest and from our hearts, but it is also a surefire way to make a woman sprint in the opposite direction. You just don't seem to want to know so much, so quickly.

Those of us who have been trained (by you) to fight the instinct to make our affections known, won't send flowers to your office. It seems like too much. And phone calls just to chat aren't typical male style. So that leaves only one legitimate alternative for letting you know that our first date was a real winner: asking you out on another one. As soon as possible. But not *too* soon.

Most men know that the first cardinal sin of dating is over-enthusiasm. You seem to like us more when you sense our unavailability. Or to be more specific, guys who play hard to get seem to be a lot more popular than ones who play it straight.

One reliable, firm fast rule of romance is this: We all want the person we can't have, and politely turn our backs on the ones who want us most. You can scream that this isn't true, but we know it is. We've heard it a thousand times from "friend-girls" who tell us about their dates. "God he was so wonderful," they say. "I really liked him. Why hasn't he called me back in two months? I'd go out with him tomorrow if he gave me ten minutes notice!" But ask them about the guy who lets them know straight off how he feels, and they mumble, "Oh. Him. He was okay. But he was coming on way too strong."

It's back to the old chemistry lesson. For some reason, both men and women fall inextricably in love with the wrong person at least once in their lives. Either single people secrete a hormone that operates like a built-in masochism gene, or they really do believe that "playing the game" is half the fun.

Let me clarify up front that there is a huge difference between playing games and acting cruelly. The former adds a little zest to a budding relationship, while the latter wreaks irreparable damage. Leading on a new guy to get back at your non-commital boyfriend is cruel. Sleeping with your fiancé's best friend on the eve of your wedding is a rotten way to start off a marriage. But casually letting the new man in your life know that someone at work seems *very* interested in you could work to your benefit.

Since man's jealousy drive is second only to his sex drive, subtly hinting that he might have competition can be a great way to see how serious he really is. If a dozen roses show up on your desk from him the next day, he is sending a positive message. If he stops calling you and moves across the country, the romance may not have been all it was cracked up to be.

We all play games, subtly or otherwise. Virtually every step of the dating process involves subterfuge, coverup, delusion, or straight-out deception. Honestly, who hasn't sat in front of their answering machine screening calls, listening to a frantic date panic at the notion that they've either pencilled in the wrong night, or been summarily blown off. (It is actually rather satisfying to listen to a date squirm for a moment or two. Let's you know you're loved.) No one likes to admit that they are consciously playing games. But since we almost all do it, why not 'fess up, and figure out how to make them work towards solidifying a new love affair.

The notion of playing "hard to get" seems to be instilled in women from a very early age. You turned your cheek when we tried to kiss you in seventh grade. You stopped us at every awkward, fumbling (and extremely painful) stage of our sexual development. And even after we are allegedly grown up, you generally make our romantic lives impossible. Sure, there is that occasional tumbling, spinning, dizzying plummet into passionate love, and maybe for the lucky few, there is no game-playing at all. But for those of us wrapped up in the dating game, there is a thick book of rules that we end up adhering to, time after time.

Lesson Number One: There is a limited amount of time and effort we're willing to put into the chase (and only so much humiliation we can take.) The rule of thumb is, "Three strikes and yer out!"

(Yes, it all comes back to baseball for men.) Kevin, a Chicago engineer, had a blind date with Jackie, a TV production assistant. The key moment of the evening? After a long dinner, he suggested drinks and music afterwards, and instead of begging off because of the late hour, she readily agreed. Kevin eventually brought Jackie home at 3:00 a.m. and left her with a nice kiss and a promise to call. This was a good date, the kind that men go home from whistling and dreaming of long weekends together.

Kevin waited one day—which he had found to be the appropriate amount of time before calling someone he liked. He phoned Jackie at work, not home—which had also proven effective in the past. Jackie thanked him for a great evening, but begged off for drinks that night. Kevin felt the first pangs of insecurity. He called a second time the following Monday, and tried to set up a weekday dinner date. But Jackie balked again, claiming a heavy work load. On his third attempt, Kevin pulled out all the stops and asked her out for a Saturday night. Jackie said she'd love to, but had friends coming into town. For a Cubs game! Strike three!

Kevin was keenly disappointed because he thought they'd had a great time on their first date. Even if Jackie's excuses were valid, they were not weighty enough to convince Kevin that she had much interest in pursuing him further. Dead relatives, business trips, and major surgery are all good excuses to blow off a date. But working late is pretty shaky. If you cared about us even a little, you might at least suggest an alternative: a late drink or dinner another night. And turning us down to hang out with your college friends is a complete no-go. You might as well come right out and say that you felt no sparks at all and would rather do laundry or pay bills than see us.

Three rejections in ten days will convince any man that you don't like him enough to date him again. This will not inspire us to beg and grovel for more.

Social misfits aside, there should be no such thing as "coming on too strong." If a man is dead wrong, don't go out with him. But if you like a guy, or even think you might be attracted, give him a chance. Don't make us play games forever. Show a little affection. Send us flowers (a bunch of wilted daisies left by the front door would be fine). Or at least humor us while we gush a bit about how wonderful you are. Many a potential romance has run aground because a hardened woman did not appreciate a little genuine attention from a slightly overeager man.

We're not asking the world of you. We can put up with the games, suffer the occasional rejection, and still show up in a blazer and jeans, hoping the next woman we meet will be the one who jolts us out of dating mode and into a relationship. We only ask that you leave us our sports, laugh at our jokes, put up with our fumbled premature passes, and give us a sign, any sign, that you had an okay time last night and might want us to call again.

Whether you are truly busy or just playing hard to get, a man is always going to assume the latter. We know in our guts that you are going to make it difficult for us to win you over. This is part of the fun of the chase, and as long as it's done with a sense of fair play, we will keep coming back for more. But we need to have a feeling that even as you seem to be dashing our hopes, in reality you are thinking about us and fervently hoping that we will call again soon. (And for the record, this lesson works both ways. If you think you've been on a fine date and the man has not called you back for a repeat performance within a week, consider his silence a gloomy harbinger of things to come. In most cases, if he really did have a swell time, he would at least resort to answering machine tag to leave word: "Say, Maryann, great time the other night. Hope we can get together again soon. I'm off to Bangkok for three weeks on business, though. So I'll call when I'm back in town. Bye!")

Decent men are surprisingly sincere in expressing their intentions, at least when their intentions are good. We can be a bit inhumane when they're not, however. We just haven't found a polite way to tell you that we did not have a good time. Ignoring you labels us a jerk. Being brutally honest labels us a pig.

Lust or Love: Reading the Signals

No matter how nice a guy is or how sensitive he might seem, one of his prime objectives during a date is to get you into bed. We will bend over backwards trying to accomplish this, even if we don't necessarily see a lengthy relationship in the future. That doesn't mean we're incapable of falling in love with you. But chances are that long before that happens, we'll be driven by lust. And we're not the only ones.

Karen met Paul at a small dinner party in Pittsburgh. The wine was flowing, the mood was right, and Karen suggested to Paul that he was too drunk to drive. She brought him home, made love to him, and they both fell asleep, total strangers tangled in the sheets. The next morning there was no conversation and no shared breakfast, although Karen did make love to Paul again at dawn. When the interlude had played itself out, her attitude was unmistakable: He could leave any old time he liked. The party was over. Granted, Paul was a little surprised at her total lack of emotional involvement in what had seemed a very enjoyable evening. But then again, Karen had not hidden her intentions. He was available. She was available. A good time was had by all. Then, they shook hands and went their separate ways.

So there it is. Some women really do just want to have sex for sex's sake. No commitment, no relationship, no big deal. We men aren't going to complain too much about this. And there is no reason why two newly acquainted, consenting (and, hopefully, safe-sex-oriented) adults can't make a beeline for the bedroom now and then. Contrary to popular belief, however, not all men are in a raging hurry to consummate a new relationship.

Julian, a Miami sports publicist, had his eye on Pam, a client from a local team's head office, for months. Their flirtation had been conducted over business lunches and suggestive phone calls. When Pam finally took the lead and asked Julian out on a bona fide date, he accepted. Pam paid for dinner, took him out for drinks, invited him up to her apartment, lowered the lights, poured the brandy, and threw herself on top of him like a cheap suit. And believe it or not, after a few moments of heavy tussling, Julian called off the whole affair. After all those months of suggestiveness, the thrill was somehow dulled by the notion of having sex on their first date.

Sure, it was a turn-on that Pam took the lead. But, in this instance, Julian felt that he'd been pushed too far, too soon. No matter how driven by their libidos men may seem to be, there are still plenty of guys who like women to resist a little on their early dates. It isn't so much that you need to prove that you live by some old-fashioned moral code (though it's fine if you do). But if the truth be known, some men like to feel as if they're "chasing" you until the last possible moment.

Occasionally, leading a man on can be a good thing. Necking recklessly with our hands all over each other in the hallway outside your door can be more than a little arousing. But there's a lot to be said for sending a man home with a surreptitiously concealed erection and head full of lurid thoughts for the next date. We like anticipation. We chomp at the bit the second we see your *Victoria's Secret* catalog indiscreetly tossed beneath the *Newsweek* on the coffee table. We wonder which bra you have on at that very moment. If you send us home without a clue, rest assured, we're going to keep coming back until we find out.

Basically, you have the ability to drive us wild. To cope with this, your mission is twofold: (1) figure out if you want to go to bed with the guy you're dating; (2) decide when you want that special event to occur, so you can be sure you're sending out the right signals. In addition, unless you don't think twice about sleeping with whomever you like, whenever you like, you'll want to become familiar with a few of our strategies as well.

First of all, with the exception of true slobs,

there's no correlation between the amount of money a man spends on a date and his expectations. We do not select the most expensive restaurant based on the notion that you will be so impressed you'll go to bed with us. And you don't have to say no to a date who has third-row seats to the ballet because you're apprehensive about the payback he'll expect. In this day and age, we just don't think like that. Any man who still does deserves a swift kick in the pants and a boot out the door.

Of course, the *type* of date we propose can be a good tip-off. After you've been to three movies and a couple of weeknight dinners, if your beau offers to cook at his place, bring along condoms, just in case. He's opening up his turf to you (and probably ejecting an angry roommate) so you can be alone. He wants to show off macho pictures of himself scaling Mount McKinley, demonstrate his considerable cooking skills, and hopefully get you on the couch, cue up the John Coltrane, and make his best moves. (He's thinking: "If she doesn't succumb to fresh pasta, good wine, and romantic saxophone music, I might as well forget the whole thing and move on.") The "home date" is definitely a testing ground.

Another telling scenario is the "long weekend date." This *does* depend on a man's financial well-being, and in many ways, it separates the haves from the have-nots. I've known more than one woman who suddenly reconsidered her "hands off" policy when offered a long weekend in St. Thomas. No one is going to alert the moral police over this. But, if you say yes to a little three-thousand-dollar jaunt with a guy you've been on only two dates with, you'd be well-advised to think about what you're getting yourself into.

Not every weekend date comes with a sexual price tag, though. It is possible to go away for a relatively innocent time with a good guy. A man who invites you to go camping, do some rock climbing, and sleep in a tent overnight might just like you and want to expand your horizons. Of course, he still might make a play for you between the foam sleep pads and cans of bug spray.

Generally speaking, when a man invites you on an overnight date, he's probably thinking about having sex with you. Assuming that you have already shared some lovely, long evenings and good times together, but have not gone to bed yet, this might be considered a healthy thing. But before you pack the cooler and head for the mountains, you should seriously think about whether you want to wake up with this fella two mornings in a row. It's one thing to finally have sex with someone you like. It's another to live with him for a whole weekend.

Boys to Men

For some of us, dating is hell. For others, it is a grand period of excitement and promise. But somewhere down the road, "The Chase" has to end. For many men, that ending brings on a disquieting time of change. Sure, we want to be in love and settled down. Someday. When we're grown up.

Dating recalls the best moments of our youth. While adulthood is racing to catch up with us on a dozen different fronts, "playing the field" is our way of clinging to the memory of adolescent discovery. Very little can match the quickening of our pulse when you say yes to our request for a date, or the nervous anticipation of standing in your doorway waiting to see what you're wearing. We crave first kisses and first sunrises, exploring the unknown with someone who heretofore appeared only in our fantasies.

Locked in the joys of the chase, we try to imagine the perfect woman. We look for a laughing smile. A winning personality. An air of mystery. A spirit of adventure. A great sense of humor. Nice tits! (Okay, I had to say it once. A good body is not such a bad thing.) And when we find such a woman, we want to boldly go where no date has ever taken us. Or at least not recently! After we make it through the first and second and third getting-to-know-each-other dates and mutually decide to continue seeing each other, we men want to relax and not worry about where things are going—at least at first. Eventually, we'll have to. But in these early carefree days, boys just want to have fun, too.

CHAPTER 2:

Sexual Fireworks

What are men looking for in a sexual partner? If immediate gratification is the goal, there's nothing like an anonymous seductress and a one-night stand. Just ask my friend, Tony, and every man who was within earshot while he was recounting the following sexual tale.

According to the story, Tony, who had been attending a convention in Las Vegas, was playing blackjack at a glitzy casino and minding his own business when a very shapely and attractive young woman sidled up to him. She happened to be quite drunk, and more than a little frisky. While Tony made a superhuman effort to concentrate on his cards, she massaged his thigh and nibbled at his neck. One errant breast kept popping out of her skimpy cocktail dress.

Finally, Tony gave up any notion of playing cards, and at this woman's suggestion, brought her up to his hotel room, where she undressed herself, undressed Tony, and proceeded to masturbate to several orgasms on top of Tony's prostrate body as he watched in the smoky mirrors that tiled the ceiling above them. She then bestowed her considerable talents unselfishly upon Tony, who passed out with a smile on his face soon afterwards. When he awoke a few hours later, the woman was gone.

What is it about this sexual experience that made Tony the envy of men for miles around? First of all, the woman was a young, beautiful, sexy stranger. Second, she initiated the encounter and took charge the entire way through. Third, she personified words like "kinky," "wild," and "*way* out there" sexually. She worked both herself and Tony into a frenzy and brought them to orgasm safely. There was no intercourse, no oral sex, no worry of contracting anything from this anonymous encounter. And finally, this odd and beautiful stranger was gone before Tony awakened, taking any potential emotional complications with her.

Does this mean that men want all of their sexual encounters to involve mutual masturbation with a stranger, or expect all women to enjoy performing under a mirrored ceiling in Las Vegas? Definitely not. Sex for a man could never be defined by a single act. Its appeal goes beyond merely having sex. It includes wanting to have sex, thinking about having sex, fantasizing about having sex, and when we do have sex, making each experience a winner in its own way. A complete ten!

Male sexuality is marked by intense curiosity, a vivid imagination, and a carefree sense of adventure. We want the act to be great, but getting there is often twice the fun. Doing it is fine, but the nuances and variations in the way we do it is how we measure quality. It stimulates our desire to come back for more. The notion that men just want to get laid is borne of a time when the one thing we *couldn't* do was get laid. We were at our drop-dead horniest during our late high school/early college years when it was the most difficult to do anything about it. Women were forever stopping us at the pass or choosing older, more mature men. Even those of us who did manage to "get lucky" at an early age rarely appreciated the finer points of sex. Some of us barely knew what the heck we were doing in the first place.

But by the time your average man has reached his mid-twenties and beyond, just engaging in sexual intercourse is not such a monumental deal any longer. He's done it enough times and been in enough relationships so that the actual act is not a complete novelty. Granted, we still hover and drool over women as if we were just released from a long prison term, but that is simply an expression of desire—not need. Once age starts to temper our horniness, we can contemplate sex as a full mind and body experience.

This is not meant to ring the death knell for wild "let's both lose control" one-night stands. If we both know what we're getting ourselves into, and conduct ourselves safely (not "sort of" safely, but completely safely, using condoms always, and for everything), it *is* possible for both a man and a woman to have an unabashed good time this way. But if the truth be known, most guys don't consider that kind of night a precursor to a meaningful and lasting relationship. And based on our experience, most women who will go home with us after two beers often feel the same way.

Men have always been adept at calling a spade a spade in this situation. We meet a woman. We get lucky. We probably tell our best friend at work the next day, rating her on technique, inventiveness, and the number of hours we went at it. But the evening won't score high on romance. A woman who wins our affections through her sexual availability, or her bedroom antics, may *not* come off as someone we want to invest in a more lasting romance. This used to be known as the double standard, but today, we occasionally meet women who initiate a sexual fling as readily as we do, and then dispense of us just as quickly. Perhaps the lesson we both can learn is that while the fantasy seduction is a huge turn-on, a little restraint—a little time spent getting to know each other—goes a very long way in establishing an enduring relationship.

What Is Sexy?

On the surface, men can be as obvious as the organ we are born with (and it is probably no coincidence our appendage is on the outside for anyone to see). We are predominantly carnivores, and on first impression, our behavior may not seem to rise much above that of cavemen. We send the message that we are sex-crazed beasts. Give us strip clubs, topless bars, porno magazines, dirty movies, and pendulously endowed women in spray-paint jeans or skirts riding two millimeters below their butts. We are men and we are animals, right? Not exactly. That isn't to say that we are not guilty of the occasional voyeuristic thrill. But that's boys' stuff. It really has little bearing in the realistic world of dating and courtship, or what a man thinks is sexy.

Sexually speaking, what are we looking for in a

woman? The world is our playground, and we are hopeless scopers, but imaginative ones. Take a crowded subway car or bus. Assuming it is not February in Minneapolis, some hint of flesh might be on display. A woman in a sexy miniskirt can stop traffic. But a lot of men are gaping just because there is something to gape at.

The 97 percent of the female population that does not dress like a runway model in Milan also has sex appeal. For every man who stands in awe of the six-foot model type with the ponytail tucked into a ballcap, there is another fella who adores the five-foot-tall woman in her stocking feet. A banker friend, accustomed to very conservatively dressed women, goes wild at a glimpse of a sexy French bra beneath a severe blouse (though it takes quite a bit of subway maneuvering to *get* that glimpse.) He is impressed with the professional look, and turned on by a peek at something very *un*business-like. A pair of Levi's and a clingy white t-shirt can drive some men to ride a dozen stops past their office in the hopes of meeting the woman wearing them.

Actually, almost anything a woman wears can be sexy because it forces us to fantasize about what lies underneath. Tom, a Galveston, Texas man, doesn't even like going to the beach because he finds women in swimsuits, for the most part, unattractive. Very few people have the perfect body, and the beach is the ideal place to discover how imperfect they can be. We are realists; we don't expect you to have a flawless figure. We are turned on by the body we fall in love with, and we are not looking for someone out of the pages of *Playboy*. Denny, an attractive Brit, loves women with "big

bottoms." Way too big for Hank, who barely even
notices a derriere, but salivates over a woman's ankles. (Truth! He lives in Hermosa Beach where
Guess jeans, no socks, and tennis shoes are de ri-
gueur, and something about a slightly tan, well-
defined ankle drives him to distraction.) Chad,
another Californian, fell madly in lust with Kelly,
who has what might be described as the figure of
a man—tall and lean with slight curves. Kelly is a
bicycle racer and she works off every spare ounce
of body fat that might produce wind drag. She
wears her hair short and spiky, and dresses in
smooth, tight bodysuits. She has the lines of a
Maserati, and draws a crowd wherever she goes.

The point is, you are going to have to take your
clothes off eventually, and most men enjoy a
woman who is comfortable with that notion.
Health clubs are good, and we're glad you're
working so hard to stay in shape. But working out
doesn't have to be a suicide run. We know the
evils of gravity, and age. We might have our fun
staring at some 19-year-old and imagining bouncing quarters off her midriff. But that does not mean
we are comparing you to her. You can stay fit without having to look adolescent. Being shapely is
nice. Working at it is admirable. But being obsessive is not fun. And frankly, it's not necessary. If
you're at ease with your body and sure of your
own style, there's always going to be a guy who
sits up and takes notice.

While your appearance might be the hook that
gets us going, attitude is still everything. Some
guys are turned on by the assertive, husky-voiced,
x-rated come-on. Others are overwhelmingly
aroused by the innocence of a potential lover who

wants to make each exciting moment a delicate exploration. Of course you don't have to enroll in acting school to become one or the other. We hope that your bedroom behavior is a natural extension of the person we have been dating, and falling for. What's more, since we are planning to be your lover for a good long time, there is room for many different faces as we grow comfortable with one another.

As we trip lightly towards a sexual relationship, feel free to ferret out our likes and dislikes. It doesn't have to be "show and tell" every time we fool around. But communication counts for everything. We're aching to know what you like in courtship, and foreplay, and eventually in bed. And as we get to know you intimately, we're willing to make mistakes along the way, in the hopes that every so often we're going to get it just right. You have carte blanche to tune in to us, as well. Experiment, explore, toy with our minds, and see how our body responds. If we can *both* relate on this level, whatever lies ahead sexually is sure to be an eye-opening experience.

First Moves

For plenty of men, climax is almost *anti*climactic, in that it usually means the conquest is over. Thus, foreplay takes on a very weighty significance. And I am not only talking about sexual foreplay, but the mental kind as well.

How do you really turn a guy on? When is playing hard to get the world's greatest aphrodisiac? When is it time to throw caution to the wind? And what can a woman do to ensure that a new man in her life is pacing his apartment and counting the hours until he next sees you?

Cara, a 24-year-old editorial assistant, joined a magazine where the rest of the staff had already been working for several years. Any affairs that were going to take place had long ago been explored. But Cara still had that fresh-scrubbed exuberance of youth, plus she made every guy in the place feel like she wanted to go out with him. For six months she conducted some of the most alluring, provocative, and encouraging conversations by computer with a half-dozen men in the office, and even went out for drinks after work with three or four of them. Although she never actually dated any of her officemates, she had the entire male staff longing for her. When she vanished abruptly to wed a fiancé none of the men had heard of before, they collectively hung their heads in shame for having individually made fools of themselves.

In today's office environment, most men are more careful than ever before about asking anyone out. The notion of the office fling has to be thought out very carefully, for fear of serious repercussions. Before sexual harassment came into vogue, however, the office tease was the hottest ticket in town. There was always one woman like Cara who managed to put out enough electricity to have every man in the joint hankering for her. She wasn't a sleaze. She didn't have to sleep with anyone. Her sexy, suggestive comments alone stirred us up like hornets in a nest. That sort of flirtation is extremely heady stuff.

Men *like* provocative talk and hints at illicit sex. In the early stages of a new romance, when nothing sexual has gone on yet, you can reel in a man like a fish on a hook without ever laying a finger on him. He'll instantly spring to attention when you allude to possible future passion. A raised eyebrow, meaningful wink, or better yet, the promise of something you might do if he sticks around long enough, has a profound effect. Just try dropping a hint over dinner that your roommate is away, and you will capture a man's rapt attention. You've planted a seed in his head that he fertilizes with images of making it back to your apartment, where it's going to be just the two of you. Then he takes a creative leap and starts picturing you dragging him to the bedroom and ravaging his body.

This is a particularly effective come-on when your roommate actually turns out to be home. You'll never see a man's face drop more quickly than when Muffy appears in the kitchen making popcorn. If you really want to run with this one, invite your date in for coffee, anyway. Excuse yourself and leave him with your roommate, while you go change. Come back out in something sexy, casual, loose-fitting, and hinting of bedtime. Then keep your date sitting there with the *two* of you. Some men will stay until sunrise, hoping you'll invite them back into your bedroom to get away from the roomie. Of course, if you've plotted this out, you'll send him home with nothing but a vision of how great you look, ready for bed. Trust me. He'll be back.

Inviting a man to your apartment is not the only way to stoke his fire. There's something about fooling around in a painfully public place that drives many guys wild. Take the lead and give him one of those wine-soaked, wet-lipped kisses over dinner. Then, watch the conversation crumble as he tries to regain his composure and find his appetite. Just taking his arm as you walk can be an arousing experience. Close intimate contact of the not-necessarily-sexual kind sends all sorts of signals that can get men thinking about good things to come.

Taxi cabs offer an excellent venue for this sort of enticement. In fact, it's a little hard to imagine how man ever began to have sex before the invention of the car. We are very turned on by wheels, as well as in them. After all, it was in our parents' Buicks that many of us first had our "members" touched by someone other than ourselves or a doctor. And there is no red-blooded male alive who would confess to *not* having received at least one blow job behind the wheel (most guys can tell you the day, the road, and probably the highway mile marker where they nearly hit a bridge buttress while climaxing). Thus, even in adulthood, the car remains one of the premiere sites men go to test the waters with a new companion. Lest you doubt this, take a ride through Manhattan in the wee hours. There may very well be more activity going on in the backseats of New York taxis than in the apartments of every married couple in the city.

Think about this. You've had a fine date. Movie, dinner, a few drinks. You're at the point where he wants to invite you up to his place. Your common sense says, "No, this is only our second date," but your body chemistry is saying, "Yes, yes, yes!" Is there a happy compromise? You bet. Making out in the backseat of a cab just reeks of delicious danger. You can almost have sex back there, intertwined bodies crushed against those naugahyde seats, shirts untucked, hands everywhere and more.

Many's the guy who has memorized a complete roadmap of a woman's body during a twenty-block cab ride. Such antics are the stuff of total turn-ons. You whip us into a lather and then leave us with a demure kiss and sweet thank you. Not one piece of clothing has to be shed for you to send us home with a desperate need for a cold shower, and the desire to see you again. Real soon!

"Fooling Around"

So the games are over. The flirtation worked. You've been to dinner. The check's long paid. We're back at your apartment. What happens next? Chances are that we'll have sex and it will be good, great, or awful. How can sex be awful? Men almost universally answer, "She just lay there." From foreplay to orgasm, "fooling around" is a team sport, and we want your 100 percent hands-on involvement when you play.

It has been said that men think with their penises, and that's at least partially true. But just because this organ seems to be the focal point of the male universe (and probably the cause of all wars in the past thousand years), does not mean it's all we care about when it comes to foreplay. When we're necking on your couch, don't be misled by the awkward bulge in our chinos screaming for attention. Oh sure, it will need to be tended to soon enough, but that doesn't mean that twenty seconds after we've touched your breast you're supposed to jam your hand down our trousers.

Good foreplay is all about arousal. Intense, shivers-down-the-spine arousal. You've been getting us fired up all evening. We've probably been

thinking about what you might be like in bed since
the moment we laid eyes on you. Now you've got
us in the palm of your hand. What do we want
you to do next?

Nipples. Balls. Butts. Ankles. Earlobes. Shall I go
on? When the action's just starting to get hot and
heavy, the last thing in the world we want to do is
come five minutes after you let us unsnap your
jeans. (And you probably don't want that either.
As you may know, twenty-three seconds after a
man climaxes, he is hit by an overwhelming urge
to either fall asleep or tune into ESPN to get the
latest scores.) This is why we are great proponents
of lengthy foreplay. The long, slow tease might be
the sexiest sonata we know. Roger recalls the first
time he fooled around with his girlfriend, Alyssa.
She was, how shall I say this delicately—well endowed! She possessed large beautiful breasts,
which for half a dozen dates had remained a fix-
ture in Roger's imagination and Alyssa's bra.
Then, one night after finally allowing Roger to
happily gorge himself on her ample bosom, she reduced him to a quivering wreck in boxer shorts by
giving him a full body massage with her breasts.
She teased and tortured him from head to toe, re-
straining his arms and caressing his body with her
own. The intense sensations of this sexy rubdown
combined with the look on her face—one of pure
desire—brought Roger to a boiling point the likes
of which he hadn't even imagined for years. When
they finally made love for the first time, she had
won him over and set the stage for a sexual relationship founded on exploration, titillation, and
constant surprise.

As most women know, men are incredibly visual. Pictures in porno magazines, videos, strip clubs—they all get us worked up into a state of emergency arousal. And you can use this to your advantage—or disadvantage—especially when it comes to lingerie. Bad underwear is an absolute no-no. You know the kind I mean. Gray, stretched-out, five-year-old panties and a bra that is fraying at the straps are total turnoffs. Ask a man about the effect of panties that droop off an otherwise delightful butt and he'll recall an instantaneous letdown. On the other end of the spectrum are garters and crotchless panties and the like. There are certainly men who go for that stripper/burlesque look. But just as erotic to some men (and often more so) are tasteful, lace bras and panties, a sheer chemise slip, or almost any bodysuit from a certain well-known catalog. And for those of us retro men, a pair of snug-fitting panties and a demure cotton bra can ignite our e'er smoldering embers.

More Moves

If all goes well, we'll be busting at the seams by now. Various items of clothing will be scattered all over the living room, and you may think you have to decide—are you or aren't you? But there is still middle ground. Good old manual stimulation, for example.

There we are, wrapped in each other's hot little limbs, all undressed and no place to go. There's no law that says we have to close the deal the first time we get naked together. We want to get hot and bothered and get you hot and bothered, but we may want to wait a while before we start making love. Casual sex is not as casual as it used to

be. The one-night stand has taken a plunge in pop-
ularity, and men (yes, it's true) are often looking
for something deeper in the commitment department. We want to devote a little more time to the
exploration phase and are not so quick to jump
into the sack as we once were. But still, if we're hot
and horny, we'd welcome help. The patented, old-
fashioned, drive-in-movie-tested hand job could be
just the thing. It comes in the standard "relief" variety or the deluxe version, complete with hand
creams and two-fisted hero worship. There is
something very satisfying about having someone
do for us what we have customarily done for ourselves all our lives.

Then there's that bastion of sheer male joy—oral
sex (or the "blow job," as every man in the history
of the gender refers to it). Most men like blow jobs.
A lot! We love the way they feel. We like the
buildup. We love to watch as you do it. I can wax
poetic for pages on end about locker room talk and
sex manual technique, but the fact of the matter is,
like every other aspect of sex, a blow job is as good
and sexy and fulfilling as the administrations of
the woman performing it. In other words, if we
like you, love you, or are "in lust" with you, the
very intensely personal nature of the act is what
makes it pleasurable. There's really no such thing
as a bad blow job. There just happens to be quite
a few tricks to make an average one shine above
all the others.

Geography is one way to score quality points.
An adequate blow job can be upgraded to "incredible" by the merit of where it is performed. In your
parent's living room, at a movie, at a party. Suggest a place. We're open-minded. The car, of

course, is an old standby. Beneath an airplane blanket is a plus (hopefully there are only two seats in your row). Doing it on public transportation earns two plusses (but carries the risk factor of a night in jail). The upper deck of Yankee Stadium, a closet in the U.S. Capitol building, anywhere in Paris—all add that special edge.

Getting a bit more down to earth, though, how do men feel about oral sex with women they have been dating for a relatively short time? We accept it as a statement of sorts. Often a woman will go down on a man to culminate a good, healthy round of foreplay long before she will sleep with him. We also happen to enjoy reciprocating. However, there is a lot to be said for holding off a bit to keep us thinking, fantasizing, and walking around for days in a daze. You see, a blow job is not just a blow job. It can be very special, unbelievably exciting, and well, kind of personal. It can be just as intimate an act as intercourse, and we like it when you treat it as such.

We also appreciate a woman who handles this particular sex act with genuine enthusiasm. If you perform it as a chore, we'll sense it in a heartbeat. On the other hand, if you approach it with passion and imagination, we'll definitely recognize it, and respond favorably.

In general, when practicing the fine art of foreplay, both parties are well advised to operate under the credo, "Do unto others . . ." So, you like lingering seductive kisses that go on until your knees buckle? Guess what? So do we. You enjoy a man who undresses you like he is unwrapping the Venus de Milo? That works two ways also. And you adore having your body enveloped in painstakingly slow, languorous kisses and more? Try the same on a man. I promise. You won't be sorry.

Sex We Write Home About!

Having whipped us into a frenzy with all this foreplay, you ask: "What's left? Let's do it!" You've seen enough movies and read enough books to know that there is a certain quality to sexual intercourse that makes men rave, "She was, well, uhh, wow! Unbelievable!" Wouldn't it be nice to have your new beau say that about you?

He won't if you lie perfectly still while he quietly humps his brains out. Yes, he will still get that ecstatic look on his face, bite his lip, roll his eyes into the back of his skull and ejaculate. Such contortions are a biological by-product of climaxing, which we usually manage to do even if it seems like you've fallen asleep twenty minutes earlier. But good sex should not be a solo adventure. We want you to be there with us, sweating, screaming, and ripping the headboard off the bed with your bare hands.

There are almost a limitless supply of sexual positions that we can imagine (or read about) and we're willing to try every single one of them. But more importantly, great sex has a certain harmony to it, sort of like the good part of a Crosby, Stills, and Nash song. For whatever reason, mutual orgasms seem to be considered the pinnacle of a sexual experience. No argument here, but the chances of having them the first time we're together and every time thereafter are slim. Although we men know this, mutual orgasms have become a matter of great pride to us. We want to get it right, and we're going to eventually. But while we are practicing, if you happen to reach your climax before or after us, it might be a nice idea to at least give the *illusion* that something pleasant is happening to you around the time *we* are coming. Try a bit of vocal encouragement. If there was ever a time to call on your ability to fake an orgasm, this could be it. You don't have to stage the death scene from *Madame Butterfly*. We *are* realists. But we don't want to kick off our lovemaking with a confidence crisis either.

Of course it's a bit difficult for us to "fake" an orgasm, so we are a bit out of our league when trying to define exactly what "faking" is. But for argument's sake, let me suggest you try to achieve a middle ground between a legitimate, earth-shattering climax and falling sound asleep while we are in the throes of lovemaking. Hopefully, whatever we are doing together feels somewhat pleasurable. We will respond to your quiet moans, your gentle groaning, the speeding up of your breath. We notice the clenching of your body or the increased exertion on your part. You can reassure us, especially when we are first getting used to "fooling around" with you, by responding to what *does* feel good. It gives us the impetus to keep doing whatever it is that works. Until we know each other so well that we can choreograph our lovemaking just right, we will always appreciate your expressions of approval—until we both reach a point where the pleasure is so intense that we have no choice but to shake the rafters, no matter what the neighbors may think.

Women's orgasms have long been an issue of intense scrutiny by men, and most of us feel an obligation to provide you with one—or more—as often as possible. But the question of how many in a single evening of lovemaking can also put a strain on the male psyche. We get off on your orgasm(s) almost as much as you do. And we'll do a lot to get you there. But just because you *can* have eleven in one session, doesn't mean we are always capable of providing them. So, please, go easy on us when that's the case.

While we are on the subject: Did you know that a man's orgasm doesn't always feel the same? A sleepy Sunday morning lovemaking session may end with one that elicits a pleasantly happy moan, whereas a Friday night "haven't-seen-you-all-week" sweat match can culminate with a blockbuster that jars our molars loose. We're aware that women experience different levels of orgasm too, and those of you prone to press for multiple orgasms might consider allowing us to occasionally substitute quality for quantity. Coming together *once* in an electrifying session might turn out to be as huge a turn-on for you as it is for men. We like the buildup and we like the culmination. We're just not always ready to start over again ten minutes after we thought we'd finished.

What about sexual technique? What drives us wild? Variety. Surprise. Daring. Enthusiasm. Vocal Olympics. The first couple of times we make love with you, we're just so damned happy to be there that almost anything will do the trick. But if it looks like we're going to be together for more than a few dates, try not to let us figure you out too quickly. To keep sex from starting to feel routine after just a few nights, call on your creativity.

Try different positions. "Doggie style," for in-

stance. Lots of us love that position. It offers a new
view and gives our hands access to you in all sorts
of lovely ways we can't achieve from the mission-
ary position. In any position, hip movement is essential. You can speak a dozen different languages
just by varying your rhythm—and we can definitely feel the difference.

In addition, more than one man enjoys making
love to a woman who still has an article of clothing
on. That may seem odd, since we have spent our
entire lives trying to get you out of your clothes.
But it can be really sexy to make love while you're
still half in your suit or wearing a loose button-
down shirt and a smile. Again, men are very *visual*
when it comes to sex, and probably due to the
same gene that compels us to commandeer the television remote control, we like to change channels.
So try a different look now and then. Put your hair
up. Wear our boxer shorts. Almost anything unexpected has the potential to be exciting.

And don't forget aural sex. We like to hear you.
You don't have to bellow like an Arkansas hog
caller, but hearing your moans, purrs, and occasional stifled shrieks reminds us that you're alive,
and perhaps enjoying the experience. You might
even try talking dirty every so often. "Gimme that
big angry howitzer, you love machine," can have
an interesting effect when it comes as a surprise.
But if every lovemaking session starts to sound
like a Martin Scorsese film, it tends to lose its impact. As a rule, talking dirty works best when we
aren't prepared to hear it. A seemingly serious, sedate woman in a conservative suit leaning over the
dinner table and whispering: "I want you in me,

now!" or other suitably graphic dialogue is virtually guaranteed to drive a man wild.

To Boldly Go . . .

Want to really turn us on? What it really boils down to is keeping things fresh. Unpredictable. Most men like the element of surprise. The first few times we make love to you, you're the surprise. We've never done it with *you* before. Foreign kisses, uncharted curves, unfamiliar scents, all add up to an entirely new sensation, and we want it to last. We want to feel that every time we get aroused, we won't know exactly what is coming next.

There is no limit to the number of things you can do to keep us in that perpetual state of sexual agitation. Try turning up for a casual date in an unbelievably sexy cocktail dress, with nothing underneath. The thought of sitting next to you in the movie theatre, knowing you are nude beneath that thin sheath, has quite an effect. So does a seductive dinner or a suggestive midday phone call, climbing into the shower with us, or just unbridled lust when we're not expecting it.

Carl and Dara began their romance as a long-distance affair. Serious long distance—Miami to Los Angeles. Their sex life was fine when they were together. But after three days of intense lovemaking, Carl would have to disappear on the red-eye flight until the next three-day weekend came around. Hopeless situation? Not for two open-minded people.

They bridged the gap by telephone. It began with the usual answer to late-night longing: a coast-to-coast talk about how much they missed each other and how badly they wanted to be together. But on one particular call, Dara took them to a new level by admitting to caressing herself when her honey wasn't around. Talk about lighting up a man's imagination. The games began when Carl asked Dara if she would consider touching herself while he was actually on the telephone with her. At first she was a little reluctant. But it's a long haul from the Fourth of July to Labor Day weekend, and they soon were conducting long, achingly erotic conversations during which he would coach her through a lengthy and climactic masturbation scene. Eventually, she turned the tables and had Carl masturbating as well, so that they were both coming, over the phone, three thousand miles apart. Not only did this phone sex keep them hot for each other when they were apart, but it brought their sex life to previously unimagined peaks during their visits.

Some of you may be thinking, "Whoaaaa, way too weird. No way I'm going to masturbate and talk to my boyfriend on the phone at the same time." You don't have to. But you may want to try it once without telling him. See if it excites you. Then consider writing him a letter about what you did. Chances are that he'll be pleasantly surprised. The notion that you're touching yourself while thinking about him tends to be a tremendous turn-on.

A dash of daring is potent stuff and can be as stimulating for you as it is for us. Try taking the lead—and not just by "being on top." Try setting the stage, playing the seductress, and controlling every single step of the way. That doesn't have to

mean handcuffs and manacles. You can really whet
our appetites by coming home from your routine
job in your routine clothes in your routine mood,
and then grabbing us by the tie and treating us to
something completely different, where we find
ourselves out of *our* usual roles, and anticipating
each and every move *you* make—especially if you
have never made them before.

There are plenty of ways to seduce a man. Try a
motorcycle jacket and halter top and sweaty rock
and roll club, if you and your boyfriend are more
accustomed to elegant and sedate restaurants.
Climbed into the shower with your lover recently?
Pulsating jetstreams of water cascading over nude
bodies can have quite a magical effect. And soapy
hands can write a thousand tales, for both of us.
Next time you're out to the movies, pick a sexy
flick instead of the latest smash-em-up thriller. Do
your homework and take your beau to something
that *you* know might fire him up (a favorite actress,
or an acclaimed racy love scene). Don't be bashful
at the theater (it's very dark in there and no one
will know if your hand is on his knee, or elsewhere!). The blatant tease, or the power of suggestion that you are a risk-taker—and can be a very
wild woman on occasion—will pique a man's interest and keep him on his toes.

The fact is, there are few limits to our desire and
eagerness to play. You won't find us complaining
too much as long as we don't get bogged down in
the same old routine. Making gentle love in front
of a crackling fireplace is just dandy. And if you
want to try jumping out of a plane, strapped together at the hips, we'll probably give it a go. Finding that spark with a woman is one of the great

payoffs of the chase. Chemistry cannot be invented, but it certainly can be enhanced. And the challenge of the game is to do that while willingly embarking upon a shared adventure into the unknown.

Condom Etiquette

I can hardly talk about all this fun without paying homage to safe sex. This is no laughing matter, as Nathan, a former proponent of the one-night stand learned when he had a condom mishap with a complete stranger on a train ride across America. Disaster on the Twentieth Century Limited, you might call it. While he was in the throes of great sex, his condom broke, and he didn't discover the damage until after the act was complete. Naturally, the woman assured Nathan that she carried no sexually transmitted diseases. But Nathan was not reassured.

For the first month, Nathan examined his penis every day looking for visible signs of the more obviously sexually transmitted diseases. He visited a doctor who clinically guaranteed that he had not picked up syphilis or gonorrhea. And then, he had to wait six long, terrifying months before he could get tested for HIV (that's how long it takes before the test is able to reveal conclusively whether or not you have been infected). The good news is that Nathan was issued a clean bill of health. The bad news is that to this day he lives in fear of having sex with a new woman, including one he is seriously dating, because he does not want to go through the hell of possible STD exposure again.

Simply put, we are living in the age of condoms.

Any man worth dating is going to practice safe sex, for your benefit and his. It is now part of our culture, and we have to learn to deal with it *together*. How do men feel about wearing a condom? We love it! There is nothing more fun than getting worked up into a complete sexual frenzy, ready to take the plunge, only to have to slide a cold, slimy latex glove onto the most sensitive part of our body, and then try to perform like a champ while wearing it!

Okay. I confess. Most of the time, condoms aren't much fun. They *do* diminish feeling. And they are a bothersome form of coitus interruptus that can convince the hardiest of erections that a cold shower and a beer is a better idea. But they *are* still the best form of protection for all parties involved, and we are going to wear them. Of course, there are ways you can make that more bearable for us.

First, men applaud the woman who is up on her condom etiquette. Definitely, definitely carry them with you on a date, or keep them by your bedside—or someplace close by. If you have to find the key to your summer clothing trunk and then figure out which beach novel you hid your last condom in, we'll probably be asleep by the time you come back. (And if the one you finally produce is a vintage year, say the late seventies, and we have to run out to the drugstore in a sleet storm to buy new ones, odds are we're just gonna take a raincheck anyway!) There is nothing about producing a condom at the appropriate moment that makes us think of you as "easy." Quite the contrary, a man is going to be very worried about a woman who will sleep with him *without* a condom readily available.

Second, the number-one problem men report when using condoms is the occasional unpaid holiday their "manhood" takes while they're fumbling around with the wrapper. This does not have to be a catastrophe. It was your sexiness that got us to this point, and with a little seductive coaxing, we can overcome any momentary lapse of attention. Specifics? Well for starters, don't burst out laughing and ask, "What's wrong?" Men never react well to that. When we're making the transition from foreplay to intercourse, your best bet is to simply keep doing whatever you were doing so damned sexily in the first place. Whether you were using your hands, your mouth, your tongue, or reading us an Anais Nin novel aloud, don't stop now. If we were ready to put on that condom ten minutes ago, with a little assistance we'll be ready to return to the fray after it is in place.

And how about slipping the little buggers on for us? Even with all this practice, they can still be tricky, especially in the dark, and especially when we're in a state of excitement, since all the blood from our brains has raced south. In other words: HELP! You can see what you are doing, close up, and you can also see that they are properly in place. Remember how much trouble we had unsnapping your bra? Think of the condom as the same sort of challenge. We'll figure it out eventually, but a little help never hurts. It fact, it can be exciting! We're getting used to wearing them all the time. You've just got to help us make it an easy and natural part of lovemaking.

CHAPTER 3:

Rites of Passage

Sunday morning. You wake up in a strange bed in a new apartment, and you are not alone. Quietly snoring on the pillow beside you is a man. He's kind of cute, could use a shave, and he has one arm casually draped around your naked shoulder. It all comes back to you. A month of dates. Movies. A day at the lake. Then this. You had that thrilling feeling when he asked you up to his place that this might be the night. Dinner was great, the wine was nice, and both of you had seen the video he had rented three times. You never even got past the opening titles before you were eagerly melting into each other's arms. Somewhere in the long night you made love twice, finally drifting off into a restless slumber wrapped up in each other's newly discovered bodies.

Now you are lying there, smiling to yourself, wanting to wake him but afraid to spoil the moment. What if he does this with three other women a week? How do you know there's not a steady girlfriend off on a three-month trip to study art history in Florence? What if this guy is all charm and no commitment? And worst of all, what if he's really terrific, and you are totally "in like," but have no idea how he truly feels about you?

Not to worry. He's running through a string of similar questions. (In fact, he's probably just pretending to be asleep while he waits to see if you're going to cuddle up or silently slip on your jeans and sneak out the door.) The entire "chase" has led to this moment: the two of you waking up in bed together, trying to decide, "What do we do now?"

This is precisely when some men slip into the "Ohmigod what have I done" panic. You see, we are programmed for pursuit. No matter how strongly we may feel about you as a person, somewhere deep in our genetic makeup is this primeval instinct to try to get you into bed. Sometimes this actually happens. Then, for some reason, once we've scaled that wall, we have a tendency to become emotional idiots. You have slept with us. Now we have to make coffee for two and screw the cap on the toothpaste and put the toilet seat down. Heck, we have to be pleasant at seven in the morning. This can be a terrifying ordeal.

The onset of panic doesn't mean the man doesn't like you. But all the rules change once we consent to a sexual relationship. For starters, we've achieved one of life's four main objectives: Have sex, get married, produce children, retire. Check "sex" off this "to do" list, and what's next? Need we say more?

Regardless, before we give any serious consideration to where this whole thing might be going in the long run, there is the small issue of where we both might be going, let's say, in the next half hour. We've only spent one night together. There is a spate of unanswered questions to consider. Do you like to sleep late? Do you take your morning coffee black, or with cream? Are you a member of any radical political parties we need to know about immediately? Our first night together may be the beginning of a new relationship, or we might discover we have absolutely nothing in common.

It's nice to dream about sleeping with someone and waking up totally, comfortably, easily in love. And it's nicer still to imagine segueing straight from that first night to a four-bedroom ranch house, three beautiful kids, and a condo in Vail. Realistically speaking, however, men and women need a little more time to figure out if the relationship has "legs."

Just ask David. He pursued Tracy, a woman he met at a party, like a dog after a meaty bone. Tracy was hot! Amazing body, stylish clothes, and a reckless attitude that reeked of fast cars and trendy restaurants. David pulled out all the stops, transformed himself into "Mr. Right-for-Tracy," and eventually found himself thrashing about in the sack with her. After a couple of intensely amorous nights, Tracy was completely hooked on David. The problem was, having relieved the sexual tension, David realized Tracy was all form and no content. She was invited to all the right parties, but stripped of a noisy get-together, she and David barely had a word to say. Faced with planning a weekend, the only places she wanted to be were at the beach homes of friends or at parties, where she didn't have to be more than just another face in the crowd. Yes, David and Tracy had hit it off sexually. But try as they did, these two passionate lovers just didn't have the stuff to lay the foundations for a serious relationship.

Once we've removed our sexual blinders, we can look at you a whole lot more clearly and distinguish other key characteristics. Do we share the same interests? Are our lifestyles even remotely compatible? Was the sex any good last night? These and other mega-questions are going to determine how we view you and what path we might be embarking on.

We cheer and applaud you for sharing animal sex with us. There's nothing like a good, sweaty, no-strings-attached workout with another alleged adult. Once in a while. Safely. But date a mature man (preferably unmarried), and the odds are that either up front, or at least in the back of his mind, he is thinking about more than just a one-night stand.

Dating After You've "Done It"

After the first time you make love and spend the night together, each date takes on a new meaning. Your new beau is exploring the comfort zone with you. If you had not become his friend beforehand, he's hoping you will now. And the next few dates may well reflect that. There are lots of little logistical items that have to be worked out. Do you start to go "dutch" after a while? Do your dates become more casual in nature? Do you have sex every time you get together, and if not, can you spend the night anyway? (The answers to all of the above are yes, by the way.)

Dating is a pressure-filled activity. By the time a man sleeps with you, he's probably had it with

worrying about the next move. At last, he can relax. The ensuing weeks of courtship are apt to be
easy, casual, fun-filled, and free of the need to impress you. His timing changes. Although he still
likes to ask you out formally, he'll probably make
things a little more spur of the moment. Granted,
you both might be seeing other people at this
point, but he sure isn't going to tell you, and hopefully, you'll have the courtesy to lie if you can't go
to a movie because you have a date with a guy
your mom fixed you up with a month ago. A man
will know you're ducking him, but he can live
with that for a while. Some even get an odd thrill
from calling to ask you out at the last minute,
knowing that you might already have a date with
another man. Somehow, it makes you even more
desirable.

The way a man *plans* a date also changes. Most
likely, he used to phone mid-week to invite you
out for a Saturday night dinner and movie. As his
fondness for you grows, however, he'll feel free to
call you casually at work and ask, "Are you busy
tonight, Ellen? Wanna do something?" You know a
man is really starting to fall for you when his invitations become less and less specific. He is right on
the edge of commitment when he ignores you all
week, then calls you at work Friday at 4:59 p.m. to
see if you're free. He is testing. First, to see how
popular you are (.i.e., do you already have a date).
And second, to determine how much you like him
(in other words, will you blow off someone else to
spend some time with him). Men know this is not
fair. But we want to know that you like us a lot.
And that you are willing to drop almost everything to see us. We won't put you through this

silly ritual every single Friday night for a year. But we might spring it on you a couple of times, just to see how serious you are.

The best date we can think of when we're playing with this idea of "relationship" is the "watcha-wanna-do" date. We call, we state our intentions (want to be with you), and we actually have a discussion about the evening's plans. This is a big step for us, because we are making joint decisions for the very first time and relinquishing control. We want you to call the shots. We want to know what kind of mood you're in. Tired? Pumped up? Hungry? Horny? Whatever! We're definitely getting beyond the "just dating stage" when we can plan the night *together* instead of just announcing the plans.

Rachel, a Chicago fashion merchant, was dating Oliver, an uptight financial analyst. Their relationship was highlighted by elegant dates, expensive weekends, and some mildly enjoyable sex (according to Rachel). Oliver was more than smitten by her, but he seemed unable to plan anything but a formal evening with a predictable outcome. So when he asked her out again to another fancy downtown eatery on a Friday night, she refused. Instead, she sent him home to change into his play clothes, and took him out to someplace *she* wanted to go. They went for ribs and beers, listened to blues at a dive bar, and then Rachel took Oliver home and had her wicked way. This proved to be the breakout date for their romance. They had been getting along okay before, but neither had really let their hair down. Rachel could have been interchangeable with any other woman who wanted to be wined and dined and made love to every al-

ternate Thursday. But once they eased up on the
formality, it turned out that they had a whole lot in
common, as well as a real affection for each other.

Men love to go out on the occasional big-league
date. It's a real thrill to take you to an elegant restaurant and then whisk you off in a limousine and
kiss you and tease you and trace champagne
fingerpaintings up and down your neck as we
fumble with the zipper on the back of your evening dress. Once in a while. But that can grow old
quickly. If a man is thinking about a serious relationship down the road, then after the first few
weeks of trying to be impressive, his desires shift
to more quality time. Can we scarf down pizza and
rent old movies? Can we call you drunk from the
pub when we are out with the guys, then come
over late and fool around? Can we end an incredible Thursday night date with a good-bye kiss at
dawn Friday morning, and then ask you to spend
the weekend with us? Those are the kind of good,
casual dates that have a man memorizing your
phone number and looking forward to the next
time he sees you.

The Long Weekend

Even the most stalwart of singles eventually
grows sick of the dating game. In fact, the main
point of playing it is to never have to go out on another date as long as you live. Even so, for men to
give up the chase there has to be something you
do, or in some cases, something we *wish* you
would do, to convince us we're on the right track
romantically.

What are we looking for in a relationship? How

long can we date before we feel strongly, or not-so-strongly about you? What does it take to get us to throw out all the scribbled phone numbers in our day planners, and get serious about one special woman? A weekend-long date may provide some of the answers.

Larry and Renee spent their first weekend together on a drive up the coast from L.A. to Monterey. Sounds like a winner, right? Nice scenery, not too huge an undertaking, plenty of things to do and places to go. For the right two people, maybe. The centerpiece of the trip was the Monterey Calamari Festival by the sea on the Pacific coast—complete with jazz and art and hundreds of booths of gourmet food. Why Renee agreed to go will forever remain a mystery to Larry. Especially since she's bored by jazz and hates seafood. But it sounded nice on paper, so they tried—and failed miserably. It's not just that their interests were different, but more importantly, that their outlooks were. Larry is casual, adventurous, and someone who likes to operate haphazardly, without a schedule or plan. If he's attracted to a woman at first sight, he's willing to give it a go. Renee, on the other hand, likes order. She wants to know where she's going, what time she'll be arriving, and what to wear for dinner that night. This worked out okay on their first few dates. But once they got out on the road, their paths diverged. Renee's sense of organization completely contradicted Larry's enjoyment of the unpredictable. He was looking for a surprise around the bend. Renee just wanted to know when the next meal was. Not surprisingly, the casual ambience of the Calamari Festival was a breeding ground for their differences, and the day

was an unmitigated disaster. Their only hope for
salvation was a visit with Larry's best college
buddy and his wife, in Carmel. But any hint of a
connection between the road-weary twosome was
long gone by then. Renee disliked Larry's friend
and was rude and argumentative with his wife.
Suffice it to say, it was not a good visit and not a
good weekend. We all know that feeling of spending eight hours in a car with someone you can't
stand. It does not make for enduring romance.

On the brighter side, Addie and Roy planned a
weekend of sailing for their first trip together. They
arrived in Nags Head, North Carolina just as Hurricane Andrew made its guest appearance and
turned their carefully planned excursion into a potential disaster. Of course, men would like their
dates to work out flawlessly but things can go
wrong. Take a three-day weekend and that just
means three times as many things can go wrong!
In the path of an oncoming hurricane, Roy's romantic sailing trip was obviously not going to happen. He was ready to toss in the towel, but Addie
found the whole situation not only comical, but an
adventure. She didn't mind that every marina for
two hundred miles had been shut down by the
storm. She suggested a tacky roadside motel for
the night that had the look of campy good fun.
This certainly piqued Roy's curiosity. They found
an open convenience store, stocked up on chips,
Cheese Whiz, and beer, and prepared to hunker
down for the blow. What could be more romantic?
Well, just as the beers were starting to take hold,
and they were having a grand old time laughing at
the creaking, screeching antique bedsprings, they
had a surprise visitor. The National Guard! Evacu-

ating the entire seacoast. As it turned out, Roy and Addie spent their first night together with four hundred other people on cots in a local high school auditorium. Any couple thrown into that sort of "date" situation and comes out laughing, has a good chance of finding loads more in common as they explore new territory.

Once you've had sex, shared a toothbrush at least once, and left for work together from the same apartment, it's time to sample a bit of real life over a long weekend. Of course, it would be nice if that first weekend was absolutely perfect. It would also be nice if bosses were human, rents were cheap, and we could always reach a mutual climax. But this isn't a fairy tale, so I'll be straight about what men look for in a weekend companion: *patience, tolerance, and understanding when it comes to the unexpected.*

When it's 103 degrees in New Orleans and the air conditioner in your room at that quaint B & B breaks, your new man may not be able to fix it. If his car's exhaust system happens to fall off on the way to the Berkshires, it may not be his fault. And should he overplan every available second, when all you want to do is sip wine and hold hands on a picnic blanket by a mountain stream, he may merely be guilty of trying too hard. Yet, women can get pretty testy when things turn sour. Think of a weekend together as a microcosm of life. You *both* have to try to make it work. Seventy-two hours can be one helluva long time to spend with someone. And as Larry and Renee discovered, unless both parties are in the mood to be there, the results can be disastrous.

So, when a man invites you away for that first

weekend, he's praying for perfect weather, good airport connections, comfortable lodging, and two days of faux wedded bliss. It often works out that way. But no matter how fun the date may be, there has to be "down time." This is when we really start to make conscious, or perhaps subconscious decisions about how we feel about you. Do you handle adversity well? Are you willing to bend a little to try something new? Can we ride together in a car for hours and not feel obligated to chat every second? This is the real stuff of day-to-day living, and guys are looking for true companions to share in it all. We applaud the woman who can enjoy beef jerky and a Diet Coke in Roundup, Montana at midnight when the only place open is the 7-11. If the forecast blizzard for our ski weekend turns into forty-degree slush, we'll appreciate anything creative you find to do under a puffy down comforter in a New England inn. We are in this adventure together and compatibility is all about both of us trying to make things bearable, if not fun.

Traveling also gives away hundreds of telltale clues about your lifestyle. Men notice and judge you by them, no doubt as you also judge us. If a guy picks you up for a weekend at the shore, and you have three huge suitcases packed, he will quickly discern that the casual way he loves to travel probably isn't your style. He may also assume—rightly or wrongly—that you prefer formality over "just kicking back" in other areas of your life as well. *Where* you like to go to relax also says a lot. If he suggests a canoe trip on a nearby river and you counterpropose two days at an exclusive resort in the Caribbean, yours may not be a match made in heaven.

If these differences exist, they're going to come to light eventually, so there's no need to pretend that you want to be somewhere or do something that you definitely don't. In fact, when it comes to travel plans, men count on you to be forthright and opinionated. If we're getting set to take you to a surfing competition in Baja when you would much rather catch the Monet exhibit in San Francisco, we'd like to know before we purchase the plane tickets.

Many men feel the same way about new relationships. We want to be sure that the chemistry is right and our signals aren't crossed *before* we put lots of time, energy, and emotion into it. And why not? The fact that we were incredibly attracted to one another when we first met doesn't mean we'll get along in the long run. That isn't a crime. Better we part friends (or even lovers), than try to make a go-nowhere pairing into a lifetime relationship. "If we can't even agree on how to spend a pleasant weekend together," a man asks himself, "how will we ever be able to mesh on a day-to-day basis?" It is a question both men and women are well advised to take seriously.

The Question of Compatibility

Allan is a Catholic, and a former rugby star from Auckland, New Zealand. Debbie is a Jewish television executive from New York City. Allan is a die-hard football fan. He doesn't just watch an occasional game. He can recite stats on virtually any player right down to the new kid from Alabama with the good hands who runs a 9.3 hundred. Debbie is fluent in three languages (none of them football). *Her* season tickets are to the

Metropolitan Opera, the ballet, and the Public Theatre. Allan likes B-grade horror movies and Wheel
of Fortune. Is theirs a match made in hell? Not a
chance. These two opposites, who met while playing squash at their local health club, have been
happily married for five years now. Allan has developed a love of Shakespeare. And Debbie not
only tolerates, but closely follows and avidly roots
for the New York Giants.

It would certainly be convenient if every couple
with chemistry and body heat also liked the same
movies, listened to the same music, and agreed
that the cashew chicken at a particular Chinese restaurant was the best in the Western Hemisphere.
That can't always be the case, though. After one or
two or a dozen tumultuous nights of great, lust-
driven sex, two people may start to notice that
their animal attraction seems to be the only thing
they have in common. Does that ring the death
knell for a possible relationship? As Allan and
Debbie discovered, not necessarily.

Daniel, a Boston consultant, had somehow managed to make it to the ripe old age of thirty without a single romance that lasted longer than six
months. What was his problem? He dated no one
but financial MBA types. Not that there was anything especially wrong with them. But every single
date and affair felt the same as the last one. The
women worked in the same field and the conversations all had the exact same patina. They went to
the same restaurants, chatted about mutual friends
from the same schools, and surprisingly enough,
went to bed more or less after the same number of
dates. Oh sure, there were a few charming quirks
strewn along the way, but if you put two MBAs at

a table, no one should be surprised if the dinner patter revolves around the *Wall Street Journal*. Daniel was desperately in need of a change, only he didn't know where to begin. Then along came Leslie. She had the look Daniel fell for every time, only she was a sculptor, not a banker, and worked as an assistant to a well-known artist.

How did she win over an uptight traditionalist like Daniel? She shook him loose from his foundations and introduced him to a different world. Instead of dining at stuffy, expensive restaurants, heavy on the wine list but light on charm, she dragged him to Cambridge coffee houses where they held hands, listened to folk music, and drank cappucino. Rather than weekend drives to "the Cape" in his vintage Porsche 911 coupe, Leslie planned Saturday bike rides and picnics by the bandshell to hear the Boston Pops. She broke his habit of ordering roast pheasant or lobster tails from the local gourmet shop by plying him with old family recipes and the North End's best pizza.

With Leslie nudging it in new directions, their "odd coupling" grew into a very interesting—and lasting—relationship. At their wedding, the groom's wedding party looked like a portrait painted at the signing of the Constitution, while the bride's side resembled Berkeley in the sixties. Yet, there they were, this mismatched couple, walking down the aisle to a chamber orchestra struggling through a new-age Yanni composition. Love had prevailed.

As Leslie apparently realized, men can be molded. Some of us actually need our eyes opened and our horizons expanded a bit, especially if, like Daniel, we've been trapped on a treadmill of go-nowhere affairs, chasing down the same type of woman with the same look and the same interests and then getting the same unsatisfied feeling in the pit of our stomachs time and time again. Men are creatures of habit. We've definitely been known to repeatedly date women who are wrong for us until the right one comes along and wakes us up. Remember that the next time you find yourself in the arms of a man you suspect may have more going for him than a good set of pecs. If it seems appropriate, try a swift but gentle kick in his pants. You just may jar him loose from his rut and deepen your relationship.

Of course, you can't force chemistry. Either it's there or it's not. But a man who has fallen for your body and started to care for the person who comes with it may be willing to learn a few new tricks. Most men could stand to relax their rigid and predictable standards. If we're rap music fans, you probably won't make opera lovers out of us, but you might get us to lie under the stars in Central Park with you and listen to Pavarotti singing *La Traviata*. We are not *completely* inflexible. When you are patient and good-natured with us, we do bend. Some of us actually enjoy being dragged along to places we've never been or meeting people outside our usual frame of reference.

If the relationship is going nowhere, we'll tire of these little excursions quickly. (In fact, that's one way to tell that your days as a couple may be numbered.) On the other hand, when we treasure every moment we are with you, we'll easily warm to the simple pleasures you introduce us to, including the obscure, the ridiculous, and the untested. We'll let you lead us through the Louvre in

Paris—as long as you don't mind returning to the states and whiling away a lazy afternoon sipping cold beer, eating wienies, and catching some sun in the upper deck of Yankee stadium.

Putting Up with Our Friends

When Jack, a pathologist with a penchant for gambling that safely can be called obsessive, first fell head over heels for Betsy, a registered nurse, they socialized as a couple with a generally up-scale group of doctors, nurses, and other professionals. But Jack maintained ties with all of his Atlantic City gambling pals, as well. Because they were not the most savory of acquaintances, to say the least, Jack didn't exactly broadcast their existence. Consequently, Betsy didn't understand the late-night calls from guys named Vinnie and "the shooter," who were bookmakers looking to get paid. She didn't realize that every time Jack was unavailable for a date, he was actually barreling down the Garden State Parkway, heading for the casinos. When she finally caught on, she insisted on being included.

This was a gallant gesture on her part, but doomed. Whenever Jack and Betsy spent a week-end together in Atlantic City, he either played hundred-dollar-a-hand blackjack and totally ignored her, or took her out to hurried casino-comped dinners where he analyzed sports odds with his pals while she got unsolicited makeup tips from their companions. She was about as out of her league as a woman could be, and eventually realized it, giving up on Jack when he would not give up his gambling friends.

Jack's story is an extreme example of a fundamental masculine trait, one that any woman looking for a lasting relationship must take into consideration: the fact that men attach to their male friends like superglue. We keep in touch with ex-girlfriends. We have a soft spot for even our most obnoxious relatives. And we want you to love these people (whom you think we should discard along with our beer bottle collection and baseball cards) and welcome them into your home. Men are incredibly protective of their friendships, and a new girlfriend who is going to challenge them is sure to run into some serious interference.

We have known you for a relatively short time, and our buddies for all of our lives. As much as we may grow to love you, our loyalty at this point lies with them. It's not that we don't want you to become a part of the gang. Quite the contrary, we want you to fit in and make yourself at home as quickly as possible. But getting to know "Weasel" and the "Huckster" and "Big Dickie" may not be as easy as you think, and old habits die hard.

You know about our more traditional vices. We are hard-pressed to give up our football. Our softball league. Our racquetball game. The poker game. The night at the pub. The list is long. How are you supposed to compete? How much do we want you to be a part of these extracurricular activities? And when should you cut us some slack and let us be?

Kirk, a former University of Maryland frat rat, fell for Teresa, a Georgetown University Ph.D. candidate, whom he met at a bar in Washington, D.C. They danced the night away, got drunk, got lucky, and got involved. So far so good.

Although Kirk was already out of college and working in real estate, he had remained tight with his college gang. "A great bunch of guys," he assured Teresa. Even if a few *did* suffer from arrested development and a variety of other social ills related to beer drinking and sports. Teresa was destined to meet these men and their spouses for the first time at a tailgate party before a University of Maryland football game. Kirk, who still recalled in nightmarish detail the grief his last girlfriend gave him every time they did anything with "the boys," wasn't sure how Teresa would mix with this mob, and was a bit tentative about asking her to accompany him. But she was open-minded enough to drop the books on a Saturday afternoon in order to meet them and did her best to fit in with his group. Nothing could have pleased Kirk more. It instilled him with the comforting knowledge that he was dating a woman who was not opposed to being with his buddies, and might even learn to like them.

A few weeks later, Teresa took Kirk to a grad school party. He was skeptical at first. Not being much for the "philosophy crowd," he only agreed to go because he felt he owed Teresa a payback. However, he was pleasantly surprised to discover that "even would-be professors could talk football." The comradery that Kirk and Teresa found with each other's groups contributed greatly to the growth of their relationship.

You don't have to love our friends, or even like them (although it would be nice if you did). But it *is* important to us that you at least try to get along with them. We know that some are drunks, creeps, horse thieves, and bandits. But we love them anyway, and we have yet to meet a woman who can convince us to give them up.

Most men know that they have to be reasonable. The NBA season runs from October until June and we cannot realistically expect you to welcome twelve guys over for hoops and brew every night for nine months. But letting the boys convene for the occasional Knicks-Bulls matchup on a Sunday afternoon shouldn't be too much to ask. If you like sports and you don't mind us cursing and belching like camel herders, this can be fun for you too. And if you choose to entertain yourself in some other fashion, we certainly won't be offended. As a matter of fact, some of us are delighted when you take an evening off to be with your gang. (It makes us feel a little less guilty for abandoning you during playoff season.)

One of the best ways to avoid serious friction over friends—even if most of ours give you the willies—is to ferret out a few favorites. If you can tolerate our old college roommate, or racquetball buddy, and actually enjoy his wife's company, make sure to invite them to group get-togethers. As long as they're around, we know you'll be in the company of your choosing. We will also get a sense that you might actually appreciate *some* of our choices in friends. This has a far more positive effect than constantly lambasting us for our extraordinarily bad taste in people. We don't take kindly to that criticism at all. Tell us something is wrong with our friends and we'll defend them to the death—even if you are 100 percent right about their less-than-savory qualities.

Another questionable crew you may be asked to put up with is our "business associates." We will call some of these acquaintances "friends" even though we've often said we can't stand them. Your boyfriend will phone you at work and inform you that he's taking you to dinner with the Smorks. "Remember them?" he'll say. "Mel's from accounting?" To which you might respond: "I thought you hated the Smorks." To which he's apt to respond: "Not true. Mel tells some very good stories about his childhood in Indiana." Which means: Mel Smork *is* a slightly less than scintillating conversationalist whom your guy wouldn't spend more than five minutes with if he didn't have to. But, on this particular evening, he must.

We occasionally need to socialize with work mates, just as you do. And we need you by our sides. You make the process less painful. You also make us look good. As the bigwigs fall over themselves admiring your charm and intellect, we'll be chatting with Smork, supremely confident that our status at the office is about to improve immeasurably because we have the impeccable good taste to date you!

And your man will happily reciprocate this favor. Just tell him where to go and whom you want him to impress. He'll make a gallant effort to make you look good too.

Shake Hands with Uncle Max

With work people, being civil is enough. We don't love them and you don't have to act as if you do. You just have to put on your best smile occasionally and pretend to get along with them for a very short while. Family is a whole different matter, though. After all, if you end up walking down the aisle with the guy you've been seeing, one day they'll be *your* family too.

Unless you're lucky enough to be dating an orphan or an exile from someplace inaccessible such as Kuala Lumpur, if a man is getting serious about you, the odds are that you'll have to meet his family eventually. There are few situations more politically delicate. Whether your boyfriend claims to be incredibly close to all of his relatives, or admits that he has been in analysis for the past twelve years because of them, he wants you to love his family. You are supposed to forget that he downs a triple scotch every time he returns home from a visit with them, set aside your opinion that his upbringing was a Freudian experiment gone awry— and then try to get along with the whole gang.

Nothing is more painful to us than starting off a new relationship with you at odds with our family. Our parents especially. We have been seeking their approval all of our lives. And the only area they've consistently cared about is if we marry well and produce halfway decent-looking grandchildren. So, you have to like them, even if we act as if we hate them. It's not fair. It's not even rational. We'll rant and rave about our folks on the way to Thanksgiving dinner and still give Mom and Dad a big kiss and hug when we arrive. Then, we'll introduce you as the best thing since microwavable macaroni and cheese, and they'll scrutinize you mercilessly.

Dad will calculate your body-fat content and look for signs that you're after his boy's inheritance. Mom will not so subtly probe for any history of mental illness in your family and try to determine how many men you slept with before you met her beloved son. And you'll have to smile through this whole awkward, intimidating affair.

The pressure to introduce you is even greater if our brothers and sisters are all already married. For one thing, males are very competitive, and we want them to be impressed. For another, when our siblings were torturing us about our single status, we told them we were waiting to meet the perfect woman. Now, here you are, and you can bet we've built you up in a big way. But don't worry too much. We don't really expect them to stand up and applaud—and neither should you.

Chances are that our siblings and their spouses will seem like an exclusive club that you're not sure you want to join. And our parents aren't going to like you for about a half dozen visits, anyway. There's just no way to avoid this trial by fire. If we're dragging you to your first big family do, and you really care for us, you'll have to suck in your gut, bite your lower lip, and bear the indignities of being shown off before a tough audience. We probably have an eye on you for a long and serious relationship. If we want you to be part of our future, then we also want you to be an integral part of our lunatic family. If it all works out, you'll only have to put up with them for the rest of your life.

Exasperating Exes

Old girlfriends. We have them. You can't kill them. And they'll probably show up when you least want to see them. Case in point? Having moved in together right after Thanksgiving, Frank and Gill were trimming their first Christmas tree together

when Frank's old girlfriend, Amy, phoned. She just
happened to be passing through town, and Frank
unwisely invited her over for a drink. Now, Gill
knew about Amy and under other circumstances,
might not have cared about meeting her. And even
though it was a poorly timed visit, Gill was reasonably well behaved. She didn't throw a drink at Amy
when she kissed Frank under the mistletoe. She did
not try to electrocute her for plugging in the lights
on the tree before she could. However, three seconds
after Amy left, Gill pitched a fit, burst into tears, and
threatened to go home to her mother's for the holidays.

Gill's dramatic response probably was appropriate for this awkward situation and Frank was appropriately apologetic (for the next two weeks).
But there usually is no reason to fly into a panic
over some practically forgotten flame. Men understand that the mere mention of our ex's name can
provoke strong sentiments. And if the ex is in the
habit of making unexpected visits on a regular basis, you have every right to put your foot down.
But when someone we call a friend shows up in
town and wants to meet us for a drink, you do not
have to throw yourself off the terrace in despair.
Try thinking of her as an old chum with whom
we'll be trading a few memories the way we do
with our male college buddies. That's usually the
case.

Marissa made a concession for her live-in boyfriend, Jay, who maintained a casual friendship
with a former lover. They got together over drinks
once every couple of months, and Marissa wasn't
jealous—until Jay balked at her suggestion that
they do something as a threesome. If there was

nothing to hide, why didn't he want to bring them a little closer as friends, she wondered.

The fact that your boyfriend doesn't bend over backwards to introduce you to an old girlfriend is not proof that he's planning to cheat on you or engage in any sort of illicit behavior with her. He's *already* slept with her. He's not going to risk his relationship with you just to make love with someone he's been with before.

It is true, though, that we don't necessarily want you to become best pals with our exes. For one thing, we get real squirmy just thinking about our former lovers and new girlfriends trading notes on our sexual prowess. For another, we want to be able to talk freely about you to our exes. We want to tell them how wonderful you are, how happy we are, what surprises we might have in store for you, and more—but we can't if you're sitting there with us.

Of course, if we all meet and hit off with each other, that's fine too. Then, you'll know firsthand that our old girlfriend is a friend just like any other friend, and hardly cause for the unhappiness that old girlfriends so often seem to provoke.

The Last Fling

Jim and Fran, an Ohio couple, had been happily dating for a year, and Jim was on the verge of asking Fran to move into his apartment with him. There was just one small matter he needed to clear up. Her name was Maggie.

Now, Jim had never cheated on Fran and did not plan to. But one weekend, when Fran was visiting friends in Chicago, Jim offhandedly asked Maggie, whom he knew casually from work, if she would like to join him for a pint at a nearby pub. Maggie, who had had her eye on Jim for a long while, readily agreed, and then invited him up to her place afterwards. There, one thing quickly led to another and it looked as if Jim was well on his way to a serious betrayal of Fran. The living room lights were dimmed and various items of clothing undone, when Jim suddenly plucked himself up off the couch, buttoned up, and made a hasty exit, much to Maggie's chagrin.

Jim never called Maggie again. (Sorry Mags.) First thing the next morning, he wired roses to Fran in Chicago. He included a note saying he missed her. And he did. In fact, he spent the rest of the weekend miserably lounging around the apartment, pining for Fran, feeling guilty for even thinking about doing what he had almost done. A month later he proposed. Fran accepted, and they've been happily together ever since.

In virtually any woman's mind, Jim "got away with murder." He broke about thirty laws of faithfulness—lusting for another woman, taking her out on a date, kissing her, fondling her, allowing her to play with the curly hairs on his chest. Based on this behavior, it would seem that Jim didn't care much for Fran. However, that was not the case!

As hard as it may be to believe, what Jim did was remove one of the last obstacles littering the path of a lifetime relationship. Without spending months chasing Maggie down or sleeping with her or leading her on with false promises and continuing to go out with her, Jim got "it" out of his system.

What is this "it," you ask. A condition men develop immediately after we realize we're getting serious about a woman. Just as we start leaning over the chasm to commitment, we feel this need to fool around with someone else. That's right. After we have dated you, slept with you, grown comfortable with you, and maybe even said "I love you"—we want to go on a date with someone other than you. And not just a platonic setup from Mom, either. We're talking about a real date with a woman we've met (or had an eye for) since we met you. Someone whom we find attractive, and whom you would absolutely hate if you ever laid eyes on. Someone we have an inkling to pursue and maybe even sleep with—although, like Jim, we may not go through with it.

And that's not all. We're not going to admit we are going on this date. As a matter of fact, we'll probably lie about it. But whether you suspect a breach of loyalty or not, we're asking you to turn your head, just this once.

We are not saying, "let us cheat." We do not want to regularly go out with other women. And we are not planning to chase one woman down until we get her to bed. That's not the idea and it never was. What's more, in today's risky sexual environment, there aren't many men willing to chance picking up a very unpleasant engagement gift from a last fling. We just want one final go at the dating game. Not a sexual encounter at a bawdy bachelor party. Not an affair with a woman at the office. Not a wild pursuit of some blonde we met at a bar. Just a taste of the action; one last dip in the pool.

"It" is our need to experience the thrill of the

chase one final time. We want to feel popular and
sexy and desirable to a complete stranger just to
prove we still can. Playing the game and working
our moves is a last testament to our bachelor days,
more so than any bachelor party could ever hope
to be.

"It" is basically a reality check, reminding us
that you really are the one. And it is a litmus test
for our relationship. Part of the commitment we'll
be making to you involves staying faithful, and we
are taking our fidelity on a test drive to make sure
it can withstand the pull of another woman at 90
MPH going round a serious s-curve. Although it
may sound like the biggest line you've ever heard
in your life, the man who stares temptation in the
face and comes out, for the most part, faithful, has
just reinforced his love for you.

What exactly do we learn from our last fling?
What a pain in the neck dating is. How out of sync
two people not meant for each other can be. We remember how long an evening of meaningless conversation feels. And should we actually fool
around, we learn guilt and remorse. It's hardly
worth it.

Even though we didn't think so twelve seconds
before we cheated on you or considered cheating
on you, sex suddenly looms as this hugely over-
rated home-wrecking act. It's as if our body was
speaking a different language right up until the
moment of betrayal. But after—a split-second
after—we remember why we love you, or know,
perhaps for the first time, how much.

That other woman? She doesn't kiss like you.
She doesn't have the same scent as you, or wear
the same clothes, or do all those great little things

to turn us on that you do. No matter what she may offer up in our brief wandering, she cannot replace what time with you has engraved in our hearts.

It might help if you tried to imagine what you'd do if an attractive and desirable man made a serious pass at you. Perhaps you would put him out of your mind completely because you were already involved with someone else. But maybe you would go out with him just to see what it felt like to be with someone different. And maybe you'd let him kiss you for that same reason. And maybe it would feel so good to have someone new so totally enthralled with you that you'd actually go to bed with him. Can you imagine the guilt you might feel and how clear it might become that you just put your relationship in jeopardy? The possibility of losing your boyfriend would remind you of how much your relationship means to you and that you really do want to be with the person you love, and nobody but that person. Knowing this, could you accept a boyfriend's one transgression, understand, or forgive it?

Closing your eyes to one random date does not make you a fool. If you discover your boyfriend in the throes of a torrid affair, then dump the creep. Shred his pictures, burn his letters and C.O.D. a thousand pounds of his books back to him if you desire. But if you accidentally happen upon him lunching with an unfamiliar face, give him the benefit of a doubt. That lunch might just be the mostly innocent date that gets this "one last fling" notion out of his system forever.

CHAPTER 4:

Getting Serious

Why does a man ask a woman to marry him? Why do some men live with their girlfriends for years and years, yet balk at the concept of marriage? Why are some men thoroughly incapable of a serious commitment? If there were easy answers to these questions, there wouldn't be so many singles' bars.

Rich, a writer in his mid-thirties, had been dating Carole for eleven months. For their first New Year's together, they decided to forego all the party invites and opt for a quiet midnight meal instead. They spent the day running around town selecting a roast, designer veggies, a good Bordeaux, and a nice split of champagne. Since they both loved to cook, preparing the meal was to be part of their celebration. Carole came over at seven and they spent the evening chopping and dicing and cocktailing until the meal was in the oven. Then they curled up on the couch to watch TV.

An evening news show was running a year-end review filled with gut-wrenching images of starving children and war-torn ghettos, which Rich and

Carole watched in silence. As the anchor wrapped up the program with a heartfelt prayer for a brighter future, they turned to each other and were surprised to discover that they both had tears streaming down their faces. Rich vividly recalls that moment. "When I saw Carole crying over those starving kids, I melted. I was ready to ask her to marry me on the spot," he says.

Carole was struck by "the moment" as well. "Here's this guy I'm totally in love with, and he's getting all choked up!" she recounts. "Seeing tears in his eyes and realizing that he cared about starving children enough to cry—which most guys just don't do—made me love him even more. If he had asked me to move to India right then, I would have been on the next plane."

So what happened next? Dinner was great. The Bordeaux was excellent. The ball dropped in Times Square. And to mark the new year, Rich and Carole drank champagne, danced cheek to cheek, and made love on the living room floor. Four months later they took an apartment together.

Of course, not all love stories end quite so happily, as Bob, a 30-year-old Detroit salesman, can tell you. After months of long-distance dating, he asked his 21-year-old girlfriend Jean, a Minneapolis artist, to move in with him—and he almost immediately had second thoughts. Had they dated long enough, he wondered. Did he really know her? What if their lengthy separations had clouded his perception of the situation? The questions kept coming, but Bob chalked them up to a classic case of "cold feet," and he didn't mention his doubts to Jean.

Then, on the night before he was to drive to

Minneapolis to help pack up her belongings, Bob
had drinks with a client. An attractive, *female* client. It started out as strictly business, but there was
something more in the air. This woman was single,
available, and interested. Bob knew it, and on this
particular evening, it started him thinking about
the terrible mistake he might be making. He decided that he couldn't keep his reservations about
living together from Jean for a moment longer. So,
he called her between the main course and dessert,
while his curious client sat alone at the table. He
told Jean that he thought they should reconsider
the move. He told her this twelve hours before he
was to pick her up. And she reconsidered all right.
She never spoke to him again!

Some "moments" make marriages. Others save
divorces. Bob was not the first guy to "falter at the
altar." For some of us, it is easier to switch careers,
dive off the side of a cliff, or move back in with
our mothers, than it is to get serious with a
girlfriend. We're talking about the "C" word here.
No joke. It truly strikes fear in the hearts of men—
although many of us do overcome it.

We actually take some relationships seriously.
We even say "I love you" occasionally, *and* do
something about it. Yes, we tend to balk at the
prospect of making the transition from boys in
love to responsible adults in committed relationships. And yes, we carry a lot of excess emotional
baggage with us on the road to marriage. Yet, it's
not an impossible mission to get us to take the
plunge. We may not be conditioned for commitment, but we can certainly be coaxed into it.

A Gentle Nudge

Even under the best of circumstances, men are prone to cold feet when a relationship is taking a turn towards the serious. Sure, we're crazy about you. Yes, the sex is formidable. And it's true—we like the same music and we both love tennis and we make a marvelous guacamole salad together. But at some point, all of this good stuff will start making a man nervous. As he sits across a table from you, holding your hand, kissing your fingertips, and watching candlelight dance in your eyes, he'll suddenly think, "What the heck am I doing here?" and feel his heart pound with something other than unadulterated lust.

Is there a way to combat this classic male fear of involvement? There are certain things you should NEVER do if you are hoping for your relationship to leapfrog to the next stage. First, don't hold your engaged or married friends up to a man as examples. Whereas you might see them as the supremely happy couple, we might view them as flawed, bickering, or rushing things (and we'll probably empathize with the guy as they start to fight over wedding plans). Try not to start ticking off meaningful anniversaries like a death-row inmate scratching off days to the execution. If we are celebrating a second (or third, or fifth) anniversary with you, we are clearly involved and we are commemorating "X" number of great years together. We don't see anniversaries as a countdown. We take them as a memorial to our commitment. Please don't sulk on us just because it isn't quite *the* commitment you are looking for, yet.

But most importantly, don't ever consider using

an ultimatum to push a man towards marriage. If he's been procrastinating for ten years and you threaten him—the worst thing that will happen is he might marry you. Then you're stuck with a guy whom you probably should have dumped a long time ago. But in a less extended relationship, where the love is apparent but the ring is a bit slow in materializing, the last thing in the world that is going to get a man to commit is a threat. Any kind of threat. He might be saving his money for a beautiful engagement ring. Or he might be waiting to establish some modicum of security in his professional life. Or he might just have a grand surprise planned for your next birthday. What better way to spoil the single most important moment of his (and your) romantic life, than to pressure him into asking a question that he's spent three years working up the nerve to ask. If the relationship is good and real—he'll get around to that moment. Some guys just need more time than others.

However, there are ways to make *your* serious intentions known and take a few aggressive steps to remind your guy about what he's got (and really doesn't want to lose). That's precisely what Patty did after she and Tyler had been dating and more or less living together for nearly two years.

Patty, who happened to be five years older than Tyler, had the maturity (and chutzpah) to know they were right for each other, but Tyler was still wavering just a tad on the commitment thing. Sometimes he acted as if he might know that this relationship was the real McCoy, yet he had a penchant for backing off at all the wrong times. Holidays. Birthdays. Anniversaries, for example. At these most intimate, romantic moments when many a man *knows* "this is it," Tyler admitted to his closest friends that he was suffering from cold feet. He wanted to go the extra step, but fear of the unknown kept stopping him. So, Patty, who also had a real sense that this relationship had all the qualities of an enduring one, took matters into her own hands.

She made reservations at a country inn in New Hampshire, borrowed a friend's Miata convertible, and kidnapped her boyfriend for the weekend. When he asked her to stop at the bank because he had only ten bucks in his pocket, Patty refused. This was *her* date. She had packed his bag, filled a cooler, and made all the arrangements.

Autumn in New England has a magical quality and Patty took full advantage of it. On the ride north, she and Tyler feasted on snacks and basked in the cool October air. They arrived at a groaning, old six-bedroom bed and breakfast to find a crackling fireplace, a four-poster bed, and a bottle of champagne waiting for them. Patty's wining, dining, and seducing of Tyler began then and continued all weekend. She also took him bicycling through the village and hiking in the mountains, where the leaves were at their peak autumn colors and the apples crunchy and perfect. Not surprisingly, somewhere amid all this lavish treatment, Tyler was inspired to ask Patty to marry him.

Men love having the tables turned on them now and then. Observe the contended grin on your boyfriend's face as he sits in the passenger seat on a road trip, taking in the sights. (By the way, this also gives you carte blanche to stop and ask for directions as many times as you want). We love the mystery of having you kidnap us and take us out, when we have no idea where we are going. It doesn't matter if it is to a jazz concert or the theater or the ballpark. We just like being on the receiving end occasionally. And should you doubt that your man would go for this role reversal, try luring him into the bedroom and seducing him as if you just met yesterday. Spare no details. I guarantee that you'll get his attention.

In addition, when he is wavering between the fun and the serious, it never hurts to gently remind him of *your* hopes for the future. He took the chance of having you laugh in his face when he first asked you out. He risked humiliation and rejection when he laid that first kiss on you and started "making the moves." Now that he's comfortably ensconced in a relationship that seems to be going somewhere, he may find himself a bit short on courage. And a little support from you can go a long way. Even if he's pursued you, courted you, dated you exclusively for months, and watched the relationship grow into more than just a casual fling, he still may need a push. Just a nudge, or a reminder that he is reading your signals correctly and headed in the same direction.

Farewell Bachelorhood

There is a certain irony to the fact that men celebrate the passing of their singlehood with a bachelor party—that traditional bacchanalian ode to the end of our freewheeling sex days. If the truth be known, by the time they get married, most guys haven't had any freewheeling sex in ages, and this isn't really what they are going to miss. A more appropriate bachelor party would be held in a small apartment with a large-screen TV, a stained couch, and a coffee table overflowing with pizza and beer. This is the lifestyle we are leaving behind.

When we set up shop with you, many of us suddenly find ourselves taking on hitherto unheard of responsibilities. Like washing our sheets. Doing dishes. Wiping beard stubble and shaving cream out of the bathroom sink. It is not that we are inherently slobs. It's just that men don't mature as quickly as women do. Women replace their teen pop-idol pinups with French museum impressionist prints around the time they hit college. We'd move to a larger fraternity house before we'd part with our Michael Jordan poster. Women buy Krups coffeemakers and dustbusters for their first apartments. We invest in a single-serving microwave and maid service. Women land their first jobs and find great dry cleaners. We're still puzzling over the difference between the "warm" and "hot" settings on the washing machine.

And it is not only in the area of housekeeping that we persist in acting like boys even though we are 33-year-old men. Why is that? Perhaps it is our secret to staying young, or at least feeling young. We know we have to grow up to some extent, but there are habits we just aren't willing to lose. And fighting us too hard in those areas will reduce the chances that we'll make a commitment to you.

Chrissie and Dack, a New Jersey couple, had one of those record-breaking courtships. Eight years to be exact, with six of them under the same roof. There was good times, good food, and good sex. They even liked each others' families. But they had been sparring over one topic for years: fishing!

Dack, who runs a retail music store and works

long hours, often six or seven days a week, used what precious free time he had to go fishing with his pals. Unfortunately, Chrissie didn't particularly care for his pals—or his favorite pastime. Just the sight of a boat made her seasick. And she didn't even eat fish!

Chrissie complained before Dack went fishing. They fought when he got back. She just couldn't see herself spending the rest of her life with a fishing fanatic. But fishing was something Dack really loved. Obviously they had a problem. And a serious one at that. It's no laughing matter to ask a man to give up a lifelong hobby. So how did they resolve this conflict without breaking up an eight-year relationship?

By bartering! There was no way Chrissie was going to take up fishing, but she did love the beach. So she laid down the law to Dack. If he was going to ditch her on all of his free Saturdays, then she wanted to rent a beach house with her friends (a group of vigorously anti-fishing women like herself). All warring parties got together and organized a beach share that gave everyone someplace to play in the summertime and eliminated the arguments that had been going on for ages. Not long afterwards, Chrissie and Dack married, and she is currently teaching their two-year-old son to swim—not fish—at the Jersey shore.

But what about pastimes that aren't quite so Norman Rockwellesque as "goin' down to the fishin' hole?" Are you supposed to compromise on those too?

As you well know, men can be pretty raunchy. We enjoy going to strip clubs, for example, and many a magazine story has been written on why.

Is it a sexual surrogacy problem? Are we manifesting some sense of frustration and dissatisfaction with our lover? Is this a sign of our own subconscious fear of sexual inadequacy? Nope. We just like to see naked women! Runways full of them. Nightclubs full of them. As many as you can fit on a stage, according to Charlie, Ned, and Keith, old high school buddies who sometimes frequented a well known and rather upscale strip club in downtown Washington, D.C.

The threesome—two married and one living with his girlfriend—have devised an effective method to explain these occasional flesh palace forays. Charlie uses the "tag-along" theory and tells his wife he is going because Keith (the unmarried one) wants to. Keith waxes philosophical with his girlfriend, and employing the "it's the same as Chippendale's" argument, insists it is safe, harmless fun. Nothing more than a night out with the boys. And Ned? He goes for the easy out. He doesn't say where he's going. (He's reasonably certain, however, that his wife finds out from Charlie's wife, anyway.)

Although they aren't thrilled about their men's little escapades, all three women respond as most men wish they would. How is that? Calmly, and with a sense of humor. Why create an uproar about a once-a-year trip to a topless bar, especially when we're not hiding anything from you?

Want to know what men really do at these places? We drink. We talk. We sit through perhaps three dances. And then, predictably, the girls all start to look the same. That's when we get up and leave, find a sports bar, watch a game, and have a nightcap with the boys. Not exactly mortal sins.

We could understand your outrage if we were going to strip clubs fives times a week or sneaking around behind your back. But once in a while, when we're completely upfront about it, we'd hope that you'd be pleased that we're forthright about our whereabouts. Granted, this might not be the cleanest of fun, nor win us any awards for maturity. But we're not doing it to hurt you. And what if we were to reverse the roles?

If you and your girlfriends announce that you are going out to a club, most men couldn't care less. Chances are that we wouldn't even object. Why should we care if you want a night out with your friends? And if you're feeling a little playful and randy and you want to see a bunch of muscle-bound apes flex their pecs, we won't complain. It only seems like fair play to us.

A trickier subject as our bachelor days wane is the infrequent, but ever-so-valued *weekend* away with the boys. Be it a ski trip or a junket to the NCAA Final Four, going away with the guys is something we've done for all of our years as singles. No one questioned us—not even you, when we first started dating. Back then, if we had plans to vanish for a weekend, you said, "Have fun. Don't mess around with any cute girls!" And, believe it or not, we didn't. But now that we are in a relationship, we know that we can't ditch you *every* weekend to go golfing. That wouldn't say much for our relationship. But occasionally something will come up that we really want to do.

It did for Eric when his best friend Trey turned up with two free tickets to Las Vegas and invited Eric along. While Trey had remained perpetually single, Eric had been married for five years, and his wife,

Jenny, was a tad nervous about letting him go. Something felt wrong about sending her husband off to "sin city" with a guy on the prowl. On the other hand, she had no reason not to trust Eric. She also realized that Eric and Trey had not spent a weekend together—just the two of them—in over five years. So she cut her husband loose for forty-eight hours and wished him Godspeed!

As it turned out, Jenny (whose unselfish act got her voted "Most Valuable Wife of the Year" by a panel of Eric and Trey's friends) had nothing to worry about. The two men winged their way to Vegas. They lounged by the pool, won a few dollars at the sports book, and got crushed at the blackjack tables. But they got to spend forty-eight hours together drinking beer and smoking cigarettes and talking about life. Men like to do this every so often. It doesn't mean that we don't love you. It doesn't mean that we need to get away from you or want to have sex with someone else. It's simply the way we choose to relate to one another. Just because we pick some rather questionable venues to do our bonding (casinos, strip clubs, and bars), does not mean that we get completely disgusting every time we are together. It's just that we have been going to these places for years and it seems natural to return to our former digs when we're catching up with old friends.

The things we cling to may seem trivial or foolish to you, but they might be the glue that holds us together through the daily grind. Men *never* call their male-bonding time "Boys Night Out." That rings of a celebration, or some grand planned evening of debauchery. Most often, we slip out with our best friend or a few of the guys mainly to talk—about the stress of work, or the pressures of making ends meet, or perhaps the ups and downs of our current relationship. It's our way of letting off steam. No one's asking you to put up with a guy who goes to the bar six nights a week, or disappears on a three-day bender because he had a bad day at the office. But do try to understand that the bachelor life we have been living is something we've been accustomed to for many many years. It's in our blood and it's not easy to divorce ourselves from it.

A lot of us loved being bachelors. Although most of us grow up and grow out of this phase of our lives, the transition can be bumpy. We're teetering on a precipice with our presumably carefree boyhood days behind us and the responsibilities of adulthood just ahead. We are giving up closets full of old habits to begin new ones with you, and we beg your indulgence. Allow us our occasional night out with the fellas. We'll allow you yours. Let us keep our Sports Illustrated collection. We'll put up with your stuffed animals on the bed. And please, just once in a while, let us act like the dopes we used to be. We'll reward you in time, by behaving like the adults we plan to become.

Fear of the C Word

Somewhere along the way, "commitment" became a locker-room term. Something we talked about with utter disdain. Something you wanted, and we wanted nothing to do with. Then fear of it evolved into a crutch, a panacea. "You're a nice girl, June," we might say, "but I've got a problem with commitment." Or, "I enjoyed last night Ellie, but you know,

I don't do that 'commitment' thing." And we're off the hook. Where did we ever dream up this excuse to avoid getting serious? And why did you ever start letting us get away with it?

Take the long-distance relationship, for example. To a man afraid of commitment, it's the ultimate luxury. Since he only gets to see you on weekends or vacations, the thrill of each reunion offers a nearly constant high. Both of you are in a perpetual state of horniness and that makes for fantastic sex. But best of all, long-distance lovers get to reap all of the benefits of an intimate relationship without getting bogged down in any of life's banalities. Laundry, parking tickets, rent, or taking the dog to the vet never come up for discussion. You just sail along in the calm waters of a new romance that isn't really all that new anymore.

That's what Emma, a Los Angeles native, and Cory, who lived in San Francisco, had been doing for over a year, and Cory had nary a complaint in the world. Emma was looking for more, though, and had been for months. But she was well aware of Cory's "don't fence me in" attitude and waited as long as she could before applying any pressure. It started mildly enough with Emma asking Cory to stay until Monday morning instead of leaving her depressed on Sunday night ("No can do," was his reply. "Gotta be at work by 8"). Then she tried inviting him to her family's Christmas holiday in Illinois ("Really sorry Emma. My mom would die if I blew off her turkey and fixings . . ."). And then, she committed what commitment-phobic guys in long-distance relationships consider a cardinal sin. Emma started talking about moving up to San Francisco to be closer to Cory.

Want to see a man twitch? Drop a few hints about invading his home turf when he's not so sure about making a commitment. Cory initially deflected Emma's advances with general excuses such as, "No need to rush things. We see each other all the time anyway." Then, he got a little more specific. "Gee Emma, your pals and your work are in L.A. You're not going to give all that up. Are you?"

By this time Emma should have been getting the message that Cory was perfectly happy with weekend visits, a steady date, and a strong sexual attraction. He obviously did not want to buy into the rest of a relationship's trappings. But Emma was not reading the obvious signals.

At the end of one weekend visit, after convincing Cory to hang around until early Monday morning, she drove him back to the airport for a 7:00 a.m. flight, and they rode in silence all the way to the terminal. Then, as Cory was swinging his bag out of the car, she kissed him and announced that she had a surprise: She was taking her vacation two weeks early and coming to San Francisco to spend it with him. Cory was surprised all right, but not pleasantly. He put down his bag, took Emma by the shoulders, and told her that he didn't think they should date any longer.

Talk about great airport scenes. The tears. The explanations (and significant lack thereof). The pleading. It just wasn't to be. Their romance quickly fizzled and died. That fateful morning at L.A.X., Emma got blindsided by a man who lived in terror of commitment. Cory could barely say yes to a movie, much less contemplate a real relationship. And in the space of a year, he had not shown a sin-

gle sign of changing. Emma saw all this in retro-
spect. Her biggest mistake was ignoring the symptoms while hoping that Cory's affliction would miraculously disappear.

Why are men so scared of commitment? There's
no doubt that our fear is real. It is more than just
a humorous escape clause from a go-nowhere affair. But if our relationships are ever going to get
more than a few feet off the ground, we'll have to
come to terms with the whole concept. Is there
anything you can do to get us over this hurdle and
prepare us to settle in for the long haul? Yes. If you
can occasionally accept the fact that "boys will be
boys," and you are willing to hold our hand
through this transition, you can ease us into something that might be called a precommital state.

For instance, three months after moving in with
her boyfriend Ted, Amy started clipping and filing
items from the local newspaper. She kept up on new
restaurants to check out and recipes to try, free con-
certs and photography exhibits to attend, local jazz,
upcoming street festivals and book fairs to go to.
Did she and Ted do everything Amy came up with?
Nope. Not even half. But did knowing they had the
options available keep things from stagnating during
their settling in phase? You bet.

Food was a particular area of great success. We
all get into the habit of eating the same things over
and over again. Even two people who love food
can slip into that rut. But Ted and Amy didn't. Every once in a while, Ted would come home from a
weekend jog to find Amy up to her elbows in the
sink, scrubbing Whidby Island Clams. Or pounding marbled Omaha steak. The fridge would be
full of exotic fruits and vegetables, and their Satur-

day night dinners became something of an adventure. Better yet, they both came to accept that even as some parts of their relationship grew routine, others could remain exciting.

Men's basic underlying fear of commitment stems from the meanings we attach to it. Loss, for instance. That fateful walk down the aisle is going to cost us more than our single status. We see each and every one of our beloved quirks falling by the wayside, shot down like ducks in a pond. First, it's the little things: canceling a subscription to *Playboy*, giving away season tickets, giving up the midnight runs to the local pub. Hardly earth-shattering, we admit. Yet, we are hard-pressed to part with those habits.

Then, as we find ourselves spending more and more time with you, everything about us seems to come under scrutiny. We load the dishwasher wrong. We sit up watching TV too late. We never hang up our bath towels. You may not be snippy or mean when chiding us about this stuff. But even in your kindest, gentlest way, you are reminding us that commitment means change.

You see, we've always thought we were perfect. Our sense of humor *au courant*, our hair thick, and our waists forever a 32. It's very disconcerting, even frightening to hear you, our beloved, perhaps our betrothed, remind us that we have faults that could stand a little correcting. "Oh no," we think. "Our youth is fading. It's time to start acting like a grownup."

We need you to help us keep the romance romantic. If we are spending four nights a week together, let's not get complacent too quickly or start treating each other like same-sex roommates by force of habit. Shake things up the way Amy did.

Gently! With a surprise candlelit dinner, an unexpected seduction, or two tickets to any sporting event. Give us a corner for the scattered piles of boxers and socks we've left lying around your apartment. Clear us a drawer space. It's a non-threatening way of saying, "Hey, I like you and want you to stay. You can even have your own space to mess up."

To nudge a terrified man towards commitment, you'll also need to gradually convince him that spending lots of time with you could actually be fun. Keep reinforcing the fact that just because the relationship shows signs of having an enduring future, he won't have to give up everything he has loved throughout his life. If both of you are creative and courageous, neither of you will head into marriage feeling as if you have already exhausted the romance in your relationship.

Stagnation can creep in like a tide, but no couple needs to sit there and get drenched. It is natural for both men and women to fear slipping into a lifestyle devoid of surprises. Adding a little zest to even the most predictable activities will make commitment seem less of a giant leap and more of a shared process—one that we both can handle together.

Accepting Fidelity

One night not so long ago, a man I know was seduced by a young woman wearing an incredibly sexy red dress slit two-thirds of the way up her tan, lissome thigh. Her French lace bra and panties covered almost nothing, and invited all. After studying each other's foreign bodies like Beethoven poring over the score for the ninth symphony, they made love and the earth moved. The downstairs neighbors nearly put a broom through the floor, pounding for them to be quiet while they did it for the third time as the sun rose.

Sadly, that lady seems long gone to him—even though he's still seeing her. It's six months later and he's lucky if they make love once a week. She hasn't done that heart-stopping thing with her thumb and forefinger in so long that he's scared to remind her about it. And the other night she actually got into bed in a robe that looked just like the one Alice on the "Brady Bunch" wore. Sound familiar?

Okay. We'll play fair here. Maybe he'd admit he hasn't exactly been the world's most exciting lover lately. Perhaps he did pay a great deal more attention to oral sex when they first met than he has in the past couple of months. And the faded boxers he's worn to bed every night this week aren't any more of a turn-on than her ratty robe. He'll accept half the blame for letting his sexual life wane, but that still doesn't make the problem go away.

Of all the fears men harbor about tying the knot, far and away the worst is that we will never again feel the thrill and intense passion of making love to someone new. Maybe you have the same fear: that because you love and have committed yourself to the man snoring on the pillow next to you, the excitement of having someone else caress your body for the first time has been lost to you forever. What might you be missing? What if you're giving up potential greatness for what might become mediocre sameness somewhere down the line?

Men worry about these things, perhaps more than women do. But if you try, you may be able to sympathize with how your man feels when he's on the verge of signing over his right to explore nubile, uncharted flesh. No more hungry, slurping "can't get enough" kissing sessions with a stranger in her doorway. No more fumbling with bra hooks while sprawled on an unfamiliar couch in a foreign apartment. No more massaging a new girlfriend's ears while studying the color of her hair and watching the top of her head as she teases between his legs. This is a lot to say good-bye to. A man's entire sexual adolescence.

His reluctance is in no way a reflection on you. Nor is he suggesting that his sex life is a disappointment. You still turn him on. He still loves making love with you. But the one thing yours can never be again is a completely new sexual relationship. This is a fact of life. Men just have a hard time coping with it.

So what are we asking? That you occasionally allow us a romp in the hay with your best girlfriend or cute sister, just for variety? That you go on wild binge diets so that one day you're a waif model, and the next, a vision out of Botticelli? None of that is necessary. In a different world, there might be no jealousy or sexually transmitted diseases, and we would all be able to satisfy our sexual curiosity with whomever we wanted whenever we wanted. But we don't live in that world. Commitment means you really are the last woman your man will make love to. And some of us need help accepting that this is not a fate worse than death.

You might be surprised to learn the kind of assistance I'm referring to has little to do with sex. You don't have to purchase vibrators and edible panties and a home video setup to get us into a lasting relationship. We probably like you in bed just the way you are. What we're looking for mainly is the freedom to still *think* about other women. "Forget it!" you say, slamming the front door and locking it as you throw us out. You don't want to support our lechery. We expect that reaction.

We know that one surefire way to anger you is to steal a quick leering glance at the girl at the next table—the one in the halter top and shorts. We even understand why you hate it. It is not your fault that her thighs are toned like an Olympic gymnast and her breasts are completely unfamiliar with the concept of gravity. We're not asking you to look like her! But if you catch us in the act of the quick peek (you know—the one where we pretend we're looking for the waitress, as if that has ever fooled a girlfriend in history), before you clock us with the catsup bottle, remember: we are looking, not touching! Mental masturbation does not constitute a felony—or infidelity.

If we flirt a bit too much with the sales clerk while we are shopping for a shower curtain, the odds are that we're merely tripping down fantasy lane for a brief moment. Unless you find out that we've raced back to the bath shop to get her phone number, you can safely assume that we're still your devoted, faithful lover. Do you really need to get so upset over a bit of flirtation with an attractive stranger?

As a man toys with the idea of settling down into a lifelong relationship, he becomes obsessed with his retirement from the sexual battlefield. You don't have to cut him so much slack that he becomes a menace to society. And you certainly don't have to put up with him if he's making passes at all of your friends. But most men won't try stuff like that, and we *will* eventually come to terms with both fidelity and commitment. You see, we love *you* in high heels, the sexy little surprises *you* occasionally have for us, and the catch in *your* voice right before you come. There is no way we're going to give up all that just to fool around with another woman. Sure, we might imagine it and tell the guys at work what we'd like to do. But that just serves to keep our libido alive and in check until we come home in the evening to sample the many pleasures that made us fall in lust—and love—with you in the first place.

Sharing Space

"Ma! Terri and I have great news!"

The words every mother since the beginning of time wants to hear.

"We're moving in together!" Long pause. "Ma?" Note the arched eyebrows and trembling lower lip. "Uh, Ma? Remember Terri? My girlfriend. I said, we're moving in together. You know, apartment, bathroom, dishwasher?"

"That's very nice, Son. Have you broken the news to your father yet?"

Generally speaking, when a mother uses the expression "broken the news," she isn't reacting positively. And that's understandable. Unless your parents eloped in a VW minibus in Berkeley in 1967, they might still think that "living together" represents a questionable lifestyle choice and clear lack of commitment. But parental opposition aside, the times most certainly have changed. Cohabitation is an acceptable alternative for those of us who want to take a step towards marriage without producing the engagement ring, yet. Two inescapable realities make living together a viable option. First, unmarried couples have been openly sleeping together for three decades now with hardly anyone raising an eyebrow. And second, the economy is tight. Jobs are scarce, and city living in particular is extremely expensive. If we're spending six nights a week together, why should we each shell out a thousand dollars a month to rent a shoebox studio apartment with an insect population and no hot water. Often such practical considerations get two people into the same space, and destiny takes over from there. Many a marriage-minded woman and commitment-phobic man have found common ground and carved out their futures by moving in together.

Having laid out several reasons why men are petrified of getting into serious relationships, I'm about to throw a curveball. There is something thoroughly appealing about the notion of "playing house." Once we are committed in our minds to taking this step with you, the notion is full of potential. For instance, apartment-hunting, while a frustrating process at times, has a tremendous payoff that makes it all worthwhile. Unlike job-hunting, which nets you (ughhh) a job, an apartment hunt leaves you with . . . an apartment! A home. A space two people chose together for the express purpose · of creating their own little love den.

The fun begins even as we sweat and strain our backs moving the boxes, belongings, and mismatched furniture up the stairs. This is our chance to play "Home Improvement" and impress you with all those wonderful skills our fathers forced upon us in childhood. Somehow they knew we would someday be mature enough to actually put a screwdriver and power drill to use.

Taking an apartment with a girlfriend is also our first big chance to hone the fine art of compromise. Up until now, we have mostly maintained the upper hand by asking you out, selecting activities for our dates, and choosing the wine we drank with dinner. But now the balance of power is shifting in your favor. Let's face it: The bulk of men know nothing about home furnishing.

Have you ever watched a guy set up an apartment? We start with the stereo. Surrounded by dust and crates, you ask if we remember where the paper towels and toilet paper are. We won't have a clue. However, we will find every stereo component, the stripper for the speaker wire, and all the extension cords too. In the time it takes you to run out for toilet paper and a Diet Coke, we'll have the CD player running and the whole place humming to REM and the Grateful Dead.

The same principle applies to the TV. While you're agonizing over how to fit our six collective rooms of furniture into three, we are making what we consider to be the only truly important decorating decision: where the television should go in order the allow the greatest number of our buddies to gather around it during football season. TV is the reason men move on Saturdays and Sundays. We can't unpack so much as a lamp without making sure the cable works and sports are on. No matter how cool we may appear on the surface, this is a big move, and music and sports are soothing. They mollify the wild beast in us.

When we make this move, we are counting on you (praying? begging?) to have some sense of design and space. We don't. (Remember what our old apartment looked like?) We *want* you to take charge here. Make us throw out the overstuffed college dorm chair (before it walks out on its own). Refuse to hang that Charlie's Angels or '69 Mets poster. And if the only thing that has lived in our aquarium since you've known us is mold, tell us to trash it. We are incapable of throwing junk out on our own. We need a push. If you don't take the lead, we will drown you in memorabilia and your parents will have to look at a lava lamp on the new pine bookshelves. So be adamant.

Furniture? This is your call too. You can make choosing it our first joint project. Turn it into an innovative date if you'd like. Bedding is another area where we are, simply put, lame. We always thought "clean" was a big step forward. Now that we have you as a partner, we can actually have matching sheets and pillowcases. (Dust ruffles may be asking too much at the beginning. Take it one step at a time.)

Even if you are moving in with a world-class slob, keep in mind that the most notorious Oscar Madison might be a closet Felix. It could be that our old apartment just got so out of hand that we gave up the battle. That does not mean we have to lose the war. Take our hand and lead us down the garden path to a great-looking first home together. You might be surprised to discover that we actually enjoy setting up shop.

Of course, playing house is only part of this commitment we are embarking on. Hopefully there will be more to our growing relationship than shared rent and matching pillows. But what does moving in together really mean? Is it a step towards marriage, a compatibility test, or do we just want a new roommate? If you examine the motives of friends who have chosen to live together, you will see that they rarely moved in just for the heck of it—not that there is anything wrong with that. In many couple's cases, though, there were extenuating circumstances. Financial reasons. A job transfer to another city, where they would both be strangers. Or at least once in a while, a sincere desire to take a stab at living together as a prelude to marriage. Actually, if we asked you to live with us, the odds are that we've also given some thought to the M word. That doesn't mean we are ready to make that commitment yet. Just that it isn't the furthest thing from our mind.

The largest concern many women (and most parents) express is the possibility that living together is a road to nowhere; a commitment without the commitment. Very few men think of it this way, though. To the age-old question, "If you love her enough to live with her, why not ask her to marry you?" we respond, "Not ready for marriage yet," or "Not professionally or financially stable enough." Or just not prepared to go the whole nine yards until we have silenced any remaining doubts. With the high divorce rate in this country, a trial run is not necessarily the worst thing in the world.

Let's say we are in love. And lust. And like. For six months, or a year. Whatever you consider a long enough time for a relationship to take a turn towards the serious. And we ask you to move in with us and share our lives without the formality of a marriage ceremony. Should you say yes? Should you probe us deeply about our intentions? Should you hire a lawyer before you pack a single box? It really depends on what you are looking for in a living-together situation, how much confidence you have in your boyfriend, and how long you are willing to participate in this experiment.

After dating for six months, Stewart and Mary Ellen, a Dallas couple, moved in together. This was a practical decision, initially. They were spending most nights at his apartment, and her rent was high. So why not split the expenses and continue living pretty much the same way they had been? Like any new and untested living arrangement, theirs went through several phases. The excitement of the actual move was followed by an inevitable honeymoon, when just buying a plant together was as thrilling as a weekend in Paris. After that, they slipped into that comfortable, noncommital "so-this-is-our-life" mode, where things like laundry and grocery shopping, which in a brand-new relationship might be silly, or sexy, or fun, suddenly transform into events that you do, well—to buy food, or wear clean clothes. Which is not to belittle the coziness of living together. But it can definitely tone down the romantic high.

While Stewart was perfectly content with this, Mary Ellen, after a few months of sharing Cheerios every morning, was getting a strange restless feeling in her bones. Would they eventually get married? Or would they continue to live together until one of them met someone else? In spite of her growing doubts, Mary Ellen did not push Stewart. As a matter of fact, she never once asked the pointed, and for many of us, dreaded question: "What the heck are we doing here?" Their future was shaped by an unexpected event. Her former serious boyfriend (and still good pal) moved to Dallas.

Just to be cordial, Mary Ellen and Stewart invited her ex over for dinner. They talked. And laughed. And got along. Except for Stew! It's not that he actually had a problem with this guy. He just detested him because he was as familiar with the mole on Mary Ellen's left breast as he was. Mary Ellen and her ex went on with their casual friendship. Stewart stewed, and soon decided that everything he wanted in a life partner could be found in the woman already waking up beside him seven days a week. Why wait for catastrophe to strike? He proposed to Mary Ellen—and not out of jealousy over the ex-boyfriend. Rather, her ex's presence made him realize that the woman of his dreams could disappear if he waited forever to commit.

The Road to Eternity

Women have a peculiar advantage when it comes to the subject of marriage proposals. Many of you, by the time you reach thirty, have been proposed to once, or twice, or perhaps a dozen times. Those of you who are old pros at this game have found diamond rings in the ice cube at the bottom of your drink or been wined, dined, flown to Las Vegas, and surreptitiously dragged to the Silver Bell Wedding Chapel where hopefully you weren't so tipsy that you woke up the next morning a "Mrs." with a whopping hangover and a vague recollection of the man in the bed next to you. This is not to say that women are fools for wedding bells. If the truth be known, men can be overeager when it comes to the subject of matrimony too. Many a guy blinded by love has popped the question for all the wrong reasons at the most ridiculous time.

Ben, an electrical engineer, dated Denise for six years without ever once contemplating marriage. Denise put up with him, suffered with him, and pleaded with him to once and for all get serious. But still he did not budge. Finally Denise had enough and unceremoniously dumped Ben for a fireman she met while he was out of town.

Denise was completely in the right. Ben had six years to make this romance stick. But he never believed she would leave him. So, when she did, he took it like a man. First he begged her to come back. Then he pleaded with her to marry him. Even though she refused, he bought her a titanic engagement ring that set him back twelve weeks salary, not to mention the prized '68 Mustang convertible he had to sell for the down payment. And all for naught. Denise was history. All the groveling in the world was not going to bring her back.

Women are familiar with marriage proposals, but many the decent fella has never imagined those telltale words slipping from his lips. Their implications set off paroxysms of fear. Let's assume that we are committed in our hearts. We know you are the one. But we are having trouble taking that last step. Are you still trapped in the age-old tradition of waiting for the man to do the asking? Or are there things you can do to speed things along?

You can always move. Ilene did. She had relocated from Connecticut to Phoenix to be with her boyfriend, Jamie. They lived together for a year, even purchasing a dog at one point (which had about the same emotional ramifications as if they had borne a child). And still, Jamie was not asking. Finally, Ilene ran out of patience, packed her bags, and shuffled back to Stamford.

Even if *Jamie* wouldn't admit that his heart was breaking, the *dog* (who stayed on in Phoenix) cried for it's "mother" every night. Three weeks of that were more than enough, Jamie claimed. Shortly thereafter he stepped off a plane at JFK with a diamond ring in his pocket.

For some men, making the commitment to wed is as natural as shaving. For others, it is about as comfortable as shaving with a dull rusty blade and no shaving cream. However, this is one decision we really have to make completely for ourselves. Although Ilene's drastic action did get results, generally speaking the more pressure you exert on us, the more difficult we will become. We are not always dodging the issue. In some instances, we are actually die-hard romantics. We *do* want to get married someday. But we want to ask only one woman, and we want to ask only once. The thought of asking someone we love to marry, only to have her say no, strikes terror in our hearts.

As we march through the various stages of the ultimate affair, we are constantly going through the mental machinations of how we might do the actual asking. From the sublime to the ridiculous, we've tried them all. Skywriting at the baseball game. A roadsign on the San Diego Freeway. One bold friend had a ring delivered by a male go-go dancer while his girlfriend was out at a best friend's bachelorette party (guess where the ring was hidden?). Whether we are pledging our love with a three-carat rock, or scrawling a note on a deserted sandy beach, if we are dating you seriously, then you can bet we have already asked ourselves, "Is she the one?"

Of the many ways you can drop subtle hints or

turn up the heat, there is one surefire way to nudge us to the fateful moment. Be a pal! It gets us every time. Ultimatums don't work. Driving us to jealousy with the threat of another man will most likely sever the delicate thread of our trust. Bizarre sexual favors are probably not going to hook us at this stage of the game, either. In the end, we fall in love with you for far better reasons than sex, money, or the fact that you know how to program the VCR. We want someone to share in the everyday comedy of life. Someone to laugh and cry with. We need to love your sense of humor, your great smile, and the way you look when you climb out of the shower every morning. This is the stuff that captures our hearts. Baking cookies together. Weekend road trips. Reading the paper on a lazy Sunday. Painting a bookshelf. That's real life, and it's just not fun alone.

We've been on a thousand dates. We've slept with more women than we care to think about. We've drunk twenty-seven swimming pools full of beer with our buddies. Enough is enough. Want to know how to get a man to pop the question? Just let him know that you can be the best friend he is ever going to have. That is what he is really looking for. Curiously enough, the rest of the details will usually fall into place.

CHAPTER 5:

From Compromise to Commitment

George and Tanya were high school sweethearts, of sorts. They grew up in the same town in suburban Long Island. George was definitely sweet on Tanya. The fact is, though, she didn't care for George romantically during their tumultuous teenage years. So while Tanya was out dating cute guys with fast cars, George silently pined away and remained her best friend and confidante.

Their college years came and went. George and Tanya went their separate ways. Five years passed before they ran into each other in Manhattan where Tanya was working as a consultant on Fashion Avenue and George had become an ad salesman for a magazine. They both were involved in relationships at the time, but they met for coffee in Greenwich Village the next day anyway. A month later George's high school fantasy came true: he and Tanya became lovers. They parted with their former partners and embarked upon a relationship that had been simmering on the back burner for almost eight years. So this story has a nice, simple happy ending, right? Not exactly.

They did end up dating for two solid years, and George eventually asked Tanya to move in with him. But there was an underlying restlessness to Tanya that George did not yet understand. Not only did Tanya turn down his offer to share an apartment, but a few weeks later she quit her fashion job and moved to London to study hairdressing, leaving behind an open invitation for George to come visit any time. Naturally, he was soon winging his way across the Atlantic. George and Tanya spent two weeks together. They ate fish and chips, toured the English countryside, and downed bitter in the local pubs. Then George asked Tanya to marry him and move back to the States. Wrong question, bad timing. George was summarily dismissed, and returned to the States devastated.

Six months later Tanya had a change of heart and returned to New York, moved in with George, and they became engaged to be married. End of story? Nope. A month before their wedding, George, who played jazz guitar, wrote music and occasionally gigged with a local singer named Carla, was given the opportunity of a lifetime. Carla and her band, George included, were invited to tour Japan and a half-dozen other countries in Asia. Three months of paid gigs sounded like heaven, especially since George had been growing restless in his job selling ad pages. And so, he asked Tanya to delay the wedding for half a year and join him on tour. No dice. A week later George set off for Japan with his guitar and NO fiance.

But this break up, like its predecessors, was temporary. Six months after the tour ended, George and Tanya were married at a Greenwich Village church. They rode the three blocks to their reception in a white horse-drawn carriage with their friends cheering, laughing, and marching beside them. All in all a joyous and much-awaited wedding day. But as you may have guessed, the story didn't end here.

Tanya was now a top hair stylist at a funky downtown salon. But George, who was still pushing ad space, felt deeply unhappy with his career. Although he had, for the most part, enjoyed his brief stint as a touring musician, the insane hours and rotten pay had convinced him not to pursue that avenue further. He took up cooking as a diversion and began taking a few classes just for fun. He was quite astounded when his new hobby brought him a job offer from a respectable New York restaurant, and even more surprised when Tanya encouraged him to accept it. She was certainly willing to stand by him through his career change.

And so George gave up his sales job and traded in his Armani suits for a white smock, an assistant chef's position, and a 60 percent pay cut. A year later he had worked his way through several restaurants and all the way up to sous chef. Tanya was making a fine living cutting the hair of the rich and chic. Together they were *the* hip young couple, sporting the latest fashions and living in a cool downtown apartment. George wore a goatee. Tanya changed her hair color every two weeks, depending on her mood. At last they had found their niche and settled down. But wait. There's more.

When summertime rolled around, George was

offered a fabulous opportunity to work in East
Hampton, a trendy Long Island beach getaway.
The restaurant couldn't be hipper. The pay was decent. And the job was out by the shore. Anyone
who has even spent ten minutes in New York in
the summer knows you don't pass up a chance to
feel ocean breezes and sand, rather than pavement
beneath your feet. Unfortunately, Tanya was tied to
her job in the city and East Hampton was three
hours away. While George would be cooking at
night, and cycling, sunning, and swimming by day,
Tanya would be trapped in the city dodging air
conditioner drippings, and suffocating in the subway. Not exactly an attractive proposition. But
George took the job. And Tanya got depressed.

But clearly, they were a couple either destined to
be together or too stubborn to separate. Tanya
shuffled out to the beach on her days off, and
George bent over backwards to make her visits a
complete blast. There were parties, picnics, and
long mornings on pristine beaches. During the
nights when George was cooking at one of the top
summer eateries, Tanya would come by his oh-so-
trendy place of employment and sit at the bar
reading a book while sipping chardonnay. She got
to be friends with the staff and word got out that
she cut hair at a trendy salon in New York. Soon
the restaurant's mega-glamorous Hamptons' clien-
tele was hearing that the chic young woman reading at the bar did the best hair in Manhattan, and
Tanya started getting freelance cutting jobs at airy
beachfront mansions. By mid-July, Tanya had taken
a leave of absence from her position in the city to
live full time in the Hamptons with George. She
cut hair by day, and spent plenty of relaxing eve-

nings reading by the bar, waiting for George to wrap up in the kitchen. Then they would bicycle a mile and a half down the country lane where their rented home lay nestled in a grove of trees by a small bay. And that, at last count, was where George and Tanya ended up.

No one ever said making a relationship work was easy. Sure we'd all like to tumble into love and have every date flow like champagne and every moment of lovemaking click like tumblers in a well-oiled lock. But if you think long and hard about all the couples you know, you will realize that everyone has problems. No one just goes from a scribbled phone number on a cocktail napkin to a four-bedroom house, two well-adjusted kids, and a Mercedes for carpooling them to ballet lessons. There are only about forty thousand roadblocks on the way to that particular status quo dream life.

Long before we get there, men go through several major revelatory experiences. Our first erection. The first time we figure out what to do with it. The first time a girlfriend figures out what to do with it. Then, of course, there is our first crushing heartbreak, our first apartment, our first job. Each one of these experiences is a life lesson from which we hopefully learn and mature. Every first is a baby step with the potential to take us from perpetual adolescence towards something that resembles manhood.

In the relationship game, one big emotional "first" has to do with makeup. That's right. Eyeliner, mascara, foundation, blush. This is exactly what happens. We pick you up on a third date and you are a picture of perfection. Our heart is skipping a beat over your porcelain-clear china doll face. We can hardly sit through dinner we are so intoxicated with your looks. The date goes well, and we wind up back at your place where we make love about six times over the course of the endless, blissful evening. Then, sometime around dawn, after we've collapsed from our futile attempt at achieving a seventh erection, you slip off to the bathroom. You return a moment later, climb back into bed, wrap your tender arms around us and slip into an exhausted and cozy slumber.

The revelation comes when we wake up three hours later with beer breath and a sore back. There you are, angelically dozing away. We scrub our furry teeth with our forefinger and hoist ourselves up on one elbow to lean over and kiss you, and— shock of shock, it isn't you! You've removed all your makeup and scrubbed your face, and yes, you still look nice, but damn, you don't look like the girl who met us at her door the night before. In the harsh light of the new day, we get to see the *real* you for the very first time, and if you're one of those women who uses lots of makeup to create a "natural" look, the difference can be quite dramatic. And alarming. Some guys have been known to run out the door in record time, ready to give up dating for a decade or two. This generally means that you just went to bed with a class-A jerk!

On the other hand, a man who readily sees beneath the foundation and blush could be a "keeper." You know you are waking up with a man who has reached a level of maturity in his dating habits when he appreciates who you are the morning after. He knows that all the makeup is just window dressing, like the jackets, ties, and cologne he's worn to impress you. Anyone who has ever dated knows that many aspects of the courtship ritual are, for the most part, a pretense. From the moment we first wake up together, we start stripping away the laughs and pratfalls that got us here, the highs and lows that accompanied our early dating days. And once we've peeled away enough layers to reveal some of our honest and true selves, we might just discover that we are two people destined to share every facet of our lives.

Love Versus Lust

Every man knows there is a vast difference between a "main squeeze" and a life companion. It isn't that we consciously make that decision on a first date. But there are just some women whom we connect with instantly. We get a sense that something good is happening and we want more, as opposed to some dates that have a distinct flavor of "this is going nowhere."

Keeping in mind that men are thoroughly unpredictable in their tastes, it is a bit difficult to suggest how to be the "lifelong companion type," as opposed to the "main squeeze type." However, I can certainly clue you in on some of the telltale signs that we look for, wittingly or otherwise.

Sadly, everything your mom told you about kissing a guy on a first date still rings more or less true. A woman who is billed as "easy" does not necessarily inspire an initial sense of lifelong commitment. How do I define "easy?" (And how do I do so without flagrantly establishing a double standard?) Well, since we are hardly trembling young virgins any more, "easy" is not so much whether you will go to bed with us, nor even how quickly you will. It is more of a mindset. A woman who never says no, and every guy knows she never says no, arguably could be billed as "easy."

The same could be said for a guy who has a reputation of sleeping with every single one of his dates. You might want to jump into the sack with him yourself, just to see what all the excitement is about. But that doesn't mean you want to take him home to Mama. This is definitely the sort of logic men apply to an "easy" woman.

When you enthusiastically invite us to come frolic in your bedroom, the part of our brain that can still focus on something other than how aroused we are is full of questions about you. How you behave will answer them—and determine how we'll feel about you the next morning. If we pick you up in a bar and you drag our drunken, willing bodies back to your apartment where you perform an array of sexual acts that would put a porn star to shame, we just might file your name under the "main squeeze" heading. And if we wake up together without knowing each others' names, we may keep it that way and move on. That isn't necessarily a bad thing. A torrid one-night stand with no strings attached has its merits.

But realistically, how many men think of women who are that sexually aggressive as potential lifetime companions? Nearly three decades after the so-called sexual revolution, it still seems that both men and women are pretty old-fashioned when it comes to sexual mores. Maybe we will see the day when the norm is a woman who is all hands on the second date, and a man who is inclined to say "No—I hardly know you." (I assume that will be the same day that bars offer promotions like, *"Men's Night* ... All men drink free from ten 'til midnight ...") But at the moment, men are still programmed to be the aggressor in the dating game. And we expect a certain amount of resistance to our sexual overtures. Although we feel deeply grateful when you finally slip between the sheets with us, the fact that it took a while gives us some sense that you don't take sex too lightly and you probably don't dive into bed with every man you meet.

Of course there are exceptions to the "don't-rush-right-into-bed" rule. Graham and Danielle were one. They met at a wedding party, went to bed on their first date, flew off to Jamaica on their second, and were married within a year.

Love at first sight often justifies a breakneck sprint to the sack. If we are out with you on the date of dates and the chemistry is undeniable and the sexual heat is high, we'd both be fools to ignore it. There are times when going to bed on a first date is absolutely fantastic, and utterly acceptable. Sometimes you just know that's where you're going to end up. It would be a crime not to. We will never hold this against you, especially when we both know it is right. Breaking the "first date rule" to have sex with us only counts against you if we feel like you've been down this road with dozens and dozens of men, dozens and dozens of times before. If we sense that you *don't* do that very often, then making love to you on a first date seems magical. We like to think that sex can still be special.

Naturally, there are a few other factors outside of the bedroom that help us establish how you might

fit into our future. Once we've crossed the fold into
serious dating, we want to see how you're going to
hold up in a storm. And we can tell pretty quickly.
For instance, if a waiter splashes a microscopic
drop of red wine on your new white blouse and
you go into an evening-ending tirade, it isn't a
good sign. We're looking at you and wondering
how you might respond if something really bad
happened.

Every relationship has a middle ground where
we are both testing the waters. The timing varies,
but if you've been seeing each other regularly for a
few months, there comes a point where a man has
to evaluate whether you are someone he could see
himself spending the rest of his life with. We may
not tell you that we are thinking about this, but
you'll know, because you're most likely on the
same wavelength. We're both asking the same
questions. Do we share common interests? Are any
of our goals and dreams compatible? Are we good
in bed together?

A sage friend once suggested that he couldn't
enjoy sex with a woman who couldn't laugh in
bed with him. I'm not exactly sure what they were
laughing about, but I liked the theory. It's true.
There shouldn't be anything we do in bed that we
cannot laugh about. And that notion should carry
over to our lives, especially if we are setting out on
the long haul together. We always read in magazine surveys that women are looking for a man
with a sense of humor. Well, men are looking for a
woman with the same. But we're not as concerned
with your witty repartee as your ability to laugh at
some of the daily indignities that life serves up.

I am reminded of my friend Arnie, who wanted

to show his girlfriend Linda an extra special time on the one year anniversary of their first date. So he scored tickets to the hottest show in town and made reservations at the trendiest restaurant and picked her up in his car to set out on this grand evening. A couple of things went wrong. When they arrived at the box office of the theater, it turned out that he had reserved for the wrong day. By a month! Undeterred, they returned to the car to catch a movie before heading to dinner. The only problem was, the car was gone. Towed. He had accidentally parked on the route of a parade that was just getting under way. So, they cabbed to a movie and then on to the restaurant. This not being Arnie's day, the stuffy maitre d' sat them at the only table available—romantically situated next to the tray station and the fire exit, with an excellent view of the restrooms.

How did Linda take all of this? With all the aplomb of a woman any man would like to date. She laughed at one mishap after another. She eased the tension when Arnie seemed about ready to take a potshot at the maitre d'. And she very happily accepted the engagement ring he presented her, down on one knee, in the dead back of the restaurant. Linda definitely had the "stuff" for a long-term relationship. Yes, she had the "look" Arnie liked too, and rumor has it, she gave new meaning to the joy of shower sex. But more importantly, she knew how to roll with the punches as she and Arnie got to know each other. Every moment did not have to be a flawless demonstration of his manhood. Together, they found a chuckle in any kind of circumstance.

What are some other pointers that help us separate a "main squeeze" from a potential mate? A woman who carries a toothbrush and clean panties in her handbag on each and every date is probably a squeeze. A girlfriend who takes a couple of months to ask if she can leave a t-shirt and shorts in our top drawer is more enduring. A date who is not going to last will resort to any and all excuses to avoid meeting a man's mother (and that's probably just as well.) A serious girlfriend brings chocolates on the first visit and worries the whole ride out that she has picked the entirely wrong outfit to wear.

Then there are those all-important Sunday mornings when we first start to wake up together. A woman who is dressed and brushed and on her way out the door at some ungodly hour just because she "has to get out of here," makes us feel about as desirable as a cheap pickup. A potential girlfriend will sneak out while we are grumbling in our sleep, and return fifteen minutes later with the Sunday paper, bagels, and a nervous smile, as if to say, "Hey, can we spend some quality time together?" When the match is starting to feel right, this is a surefire way to our hearts.

The Writing on the Wall

Beyond these delightful little intangibles of love and romance, there are some real life issues that can make or break a relationship. You are all well advised to keep your eyes wide open while exploring exciting new territory with a boyfriend, because these are landmines that can sink lifelong plans in an instant.

Take Lawrence and Naomi. They met on a blind

date and embarked on a fast and heady romance. They quickly became an exclusive item and seemed well on the road to an engagement when a thorny problem popped up over lunch in a local diner. Lawrence was a reformed Jew. Naomi, an orthodox one. To the uninitiated, this may not seem a big deal. Same religion, no problem. But orthodox Judaism has its own set of laws and customs that do not coincide with Lawrence's more relaxed practice of his faith.

For instance, Naomi had been educated in orthodox Jewish schools from kindergarten through college. Lawrence had attended public high school and a state university. During a casual chat over grilled cheese sandwiches (which Lawrence had already grown accustomed to eating without his beloved, but un-kosher bacon), Naomi mentioned that she'd like her children to attend the Hebrew school system from beginning to end. This wasn't a question, but a statement of fact. Since she and Lawrence were not even engaged and had never had a serious conversation about children, this was the first time the topic had come up, and Lawrence had a decidedly different view of it. He took the stance that he would like his kids to have a strong education, perhaps private school, but in no lifetime would he want to send a kid to sixteen years of Hebrew-school-only background. Naomi was adamant. In her mind, there was only one way to educate children, and that was through Hebrew school. Not surprisingly, Naomi and Lawrence split up for good a few weeks later.

There are dozens of other life issues, large and small, that men want to ferret out before we are willing to face a greater commitment. Martin, an

Australian commodities broker, fell in love with Theresa, a schoolteacher from Maine, while he was on a three-month holiday in the States. Their whirlwind romance was dashed when Theresa informed him that she simply could not see herself living in another country someday, especially one that was twelve thousand miles away from the rocky coast of Maine.

Ray, a diehard Atlanta Braves enthusiast, nixed his affair with Nan, a theatrical stage manager, because she despised baseball. This may sound silly, but Ray attends a couple of dozen games a year and watches many, many more on TV. The prospect of relaxing on a Saturday afternoon with a mate who was clucking her tongue and looking down her nose at him seemed unrealistic and unpleasant. Regardless of how much he liked Nan, he also loved baseball enough to dive back into the singles fray and find a girlfriend who was a little more tolerant of America's pastime.

And in one of the most creative breakups I've ever heard about, Eugene split with his girlfriend Carrie because she didn't like garlic! Eugene is a copywriter who spends about a gazillion hours a week brainstorming and sitting behind a blank computer screen. On a good day, he might have one idea and write six words. He loves cooking because it's a thousand miles from copywriting and always produces a tangible result. In contrast to grabbing at thin air for advertising ideas, while cooking, he can chop and dice and slice and end up with something real. Well, Carrie definitely didn't share his enthusiasm. She was a salad bar/ slice of fruit type who didn't really care what she ate. The only thing she couldn't stand was garlic.

Since Eugene's culinary passion was cooking with garlic, their romance was doomed from the start.

The point is, when we are looking at you with at least semi-serious intentions, we need a hint that we are going to get along for more than just a couple of dates. We suspect that our relationship with you could be the most pervasive and lasting and important relationship of our life. We've been stuck with our guy friends for a few dozen years, but we didn't have to sleep with them. And our female buddies have managed to deal with us, because they didn't have to live with our cute little idiosyncrasies on a daily basis. The serious contender for our hearts is going to have to put up with a lot. In fact, *both* of us are going to have to make sacrifices to keep peace in the home. But before we get to that stage, it's nice to know that we are chasing a woman who shares in some of our pleasures and joys. There's no real reason to set off on a lifelong journey if we both know that we have nothing in common. It's one thing to share a bed and a toothbrush and a few laughs. It's a whole different ball game when diaper changing, house building, and retirement planning become involved.

When the Road to Love Is Paved with Tacks

Church bells rang out over the rolling hills of a Maryland farm when Scott and Mona tied the knot two years ago. The young couple danced the two-step in tux and gown and cowboy boots as a hundred guests clapped their hands and howled and hooted and "yeeee-haahhhed" their approval. When the cake was cut and the last Bud swilled, the entire wedding party wandered to the north forty where a hot air balloon lifted the newlyweds off into the azure blue skies of their new life. A picture-book wedding to be sure. If only life could remain so perfect.

The first trauma was Mona's health. Nagging pain led to a diagnosis of endometriosis, a condition that could require a hysterectomy. Except that Scott and Mona wanted nothing more than to have children. Fortunately, pregnancy, on occasion, has proven to alleviate many of the symptoms of Mona's ailment. So the simple cure was to conceive a child. A little earlier than they might have planned, but nevertheless, the right answer. Only one problem. After six months of trying, nothing happened. Calamity number two. Scott went in for tests and doctors determined that his sperm count was extremely low. He was, for all practical purposes, firing blanks. But not completely infertile, so there was hope.

As Mona's endometriosis worsened, they decided to take drastic action and attempt the extraordinarily expensive medical procedure of in vitro fertilization. Scott's few live sperm would be matched with Mona's eggs in a test tube and returned to her uterus, where hopefully a child could be conceived. With any luck, this might relieve her of the constantly worsening pain (she was having laser surgery on a regular basis at this point). Three attempts and twenty thousand dollars later, still no baby.

Mona's condition persisted. But they adopted a baby girl whom they were happily raising. And in the hopes of having a child by natural childbirth, they were planning another year of in vitro when money allowed. After two years of marriage, one could say their plate was full enough. But still, the problems kept coming. Scott blew out his knee in a neighborhood football game. A month later, Mona had a freak accident involving an uninsured driver who turned around and filed a lawsuit for a quarter of a million dollars. Talk about the harsh realities of life? Scott and Mona could sell their story to a daytime soap and retire on the royalties. Through all of this, though, they have remained a supremely happy and strong couple. Such were the vows they took. "For better or for worse." Scott and Mona just happened to get more "worse" than "better" at first.

As men waltz through their wedding days, we ask for little more than health, happiness, perhaps a pinch of financial success—and that you will be by our sides forever. The day we walk down the aisle is the beginning of a mystery we'll spend a lifetime unraveling. Where will we be in a dozen years? Will our kids have buck teeth? Is there a remote chance that our honeymoon villa will be half as nice as it looked in the brochure? These are the lighter issues. No one really anticipates the other side of the coin. What if one of us gets ill? What if we lose our jobs? Who is going to take care of our parents as we all grow older? We can't plan for all of these contingencies. But we can sure look for a partner who has the maturity to deal with them should they befall us.

When Josh and Sarah were living together in Los Angeles, Josh bought a small Honda motorcycle—a yuppie bike—that they used on the weekends. They would wake up at dawn and race up the Pacific Coast Highway to Point Dune, make love on the beach, and then, after having a huge breakfast at a

fisherman's joint, roar down the coast and have the
bike back in the garage before the morning traffic
even got heavy. All in all, a very safe hobby. Until
the day Josh's car broke down and he decided to
take the bike to work. In rush-hour traffic, a milk
truck blew a tire and smashed into him. It would
take three weeks and two major surgeries to save his
leg.

Sarah, who was five years Josh's junior, became
an adult the day she received the hospital's call at
work and rolled into action. No panic, no tears, no
hysteria. She alerted the important friends and
telephoned Josh's father back East, staying calm,
cool, and collected so as not to make things seem
any worse than they were. She held Josh's hand for
four hours before surgery and waited through it
with no idea whether he would come out with two
legs. By the time his father arrived, she had arranged for a hotel room and a car to meet him at
the airport. Instead of a disaster, he arrived to find
a bad situation under control. And that was how
Sarah kept it for the nine months of Josh's agonizing rehabilitation—which was no prize ticket either. Aside from pain, a subsequent addiction to
painkillers, and unemployment, Josh offered cruel
words, sleepless nights, and no sex for half a year.
Sarah hung in through all of it, though. She was
also there by his side a year and a half later, when
he was physically and emotionally recovered and
walked with *two* pretty good legs down the aisle.

We might fall in love with the "little girl" in you,
but it is the woman with whom we think about
growing old. That is not to say that as you lie sexily in our bed, a playful and innocent 22-year-old,
we are actually contemplating what you will be

like when we are garrulous old men hooked up to heart machines grumbling about hospital food and pinching the nurse's ass. But there is a certain comfort in playing grownup, even when we are both interminably young and completely fooled into thinking life will be one long carnival. As we wander from first dates to weekends to living together, wondering if you are "the one," we look for the slightest clue of who you might become.

Life's little cross-ups do not have to be as dramatic as traffic accidents and horrible diseases. The daily grind provides more than enough tension to test a couple's mettle. Patrick and Donna had been dating for a year, when, over a romantic dinner at a sidewalk cafe, he asked her to live with him. She happily agreed, and a month later they found a small studio apartment in a high-rise building with a terrace. This being New York, they were poor, but happy. And after about two months of reeling from their astronomic moving costs, they finally got about twelve hours ahead in their paychecks and decided to plant a small garden on their sunny terrace.

In Manhattan, people grow everything from a couple of potted petunias to an entire cornfield in their windowboxes. Patrick and Donna chose the bare-bones route. They built their planters and sowed their seeds from cute little packets that Donna dated and framed. Then they sat on their terrace every evening that summer, watching their herbs and flowers grow. They barely had enough money to go out for Chinese food, but they could always have a pot of spaghetti sauce seasoned with home-grown basil simmering on the stove.

There was nothing particularly tragic about Pa-

trick and Donna's starving first days together.
They were frustrated, and they occasionally fought
about stirring matters like whether to eat or go to
a movie. But Patrick didn't need a crisis to befall
them to see that Donna was a woman you invest in
for the long run. Their daily unhappinesses were
of the low-voltage variety. Small paychecks, large
bills, and hot summer weekends when they sat in,
praying that their old window air-conditioning
unit didn't wheeze, gasp one last time, and quit!
Donna took every second of it in stride. No matter
how grumpy her boyfriend became over the financial struggle, she had a cheerful solution. Be it a
free concert in the park or homemade pizza and
jug wine with friends, Donna made their household a pleasant place to be.

It's that sort of gentle, warm, contented feeling
that men look for in the day-to-day realities of a
lasting relationship. It's okay to have the routine
occasionally broken by some minor occurrence.
Winning the lottery for instance. But it is just as
likely that our quiet little life will be interrupted by
something unexpected, which we would just as
soon live without. Cars break down and die. Parents get sick. Jobs have a nasty tendency to vanish
these days. We know we can handle the good
times. We are looking to see how you might survive the bad.

Popping the Question

What does it take to get a man to ask you to
marry him? There are few subjects that make men
squirm more. Just the word "engagement" makes
our whole life flash before our eyes. Think of ev-

erything we have to give up. No more sex with the Dallas Cowboys Cheerleaders! No more Lear-jet junkets to Vegas with the buddies. No more two-week bone-fishing outings in the Keys. Okay, so maybe we are exaggerating just a tad. But marriage *is* going to change our lives dramatically.

We've grown accustomed to our Mount Vesuvius of laundry on the bedroom floor. We can see no good reason to take the beer cans out for recycling until we've stockpiled a minimum of three cases worth. And plain and simple, we are not giving up our baseball card collection. We will find room. We will *build* a room if necessary! We'll make some sacrifices, but if we're to seriously contemplate this marriage business, you'll need to make concessions, too.

There are probably some guys who are born to wed. We can also assume that their handkerchiefs are pressed, their checkbooks balanced, and their memberships at the country club assured. But what about the malingerers and the chicken-hearted? What do you do about the loveable teddy bear who would carry you across a snake-filled bog or rip the head off any guy who gave you so much as a cross-eyed glance, but when pressed on the issue of marriage, develops a stutter, breaks into hives, or joins the military?

First and foremost, do not panic. If we have been dating you for a long while or we are living with you, we are probably going to marry you. Eventually. Bachelorhood is not nearly as trendy as it used to be, and old bachelors are about as common as virgins these days. We want to pop the question. We just have to overcome a few fears first. Like fear of putting the toilet seat down. Fear of fabric softener. Fear of calling your father "Dad." Is there anything you can do to speed the process along? Well, you might try loosening the reins a bit. Cut your man some slack with the fellas. Let him see how much fun life with his buddies is going to be if he doesn't get serious with you soon.

Janet was living with Chip, the original party animal. Only Chip was getting dangerously close to his middle thirties, and his single friends were dropping like flies. That didn't mean the old gang didn't hang out anymore. But instead of the weekly bash at the local sports bar, the guys found themselves getting together more often for weddings than anything else. So when the next-to-last man in the gang got engaged, Chip, being the only friend without a wife in tow, got assigned the task of organizing the bachelor party. He reserved a suite in Atlantic City, ordered a limousine full of beer and arranged for all the accoutrement a half-dozen fellas might need to gamble, smoke cigars, and make fools of themselves until daybreak.

Oddly enough, this bastion of male debauchery had a profoundly sobering effect on "the Chipster." On the limo ride home, while five of six guys were passed out snoring in the back of the stretch, Chip sat up, sucking cold beers and staring pensively out the tinted windows. Reflected in it, he saw five great friends, the last of whom was about to tie the knot, and he suddenly saw himself alone in a sleazy bar swilling a whisky and making small talk with a lonely barkeep. Chip was chilled by the vision of himself someday being greeted at the local bar as "old-timer." At his friend's wedding a week later, Chip asked Janet to marry him.

Generally speaking, subtle pressure is a much

better means of getting a man to take stock than
holding him hostage and dragging him to a jew-
eler. Which is not to say that you have to wait for
an entire fraternity house to wed before your man
makes up his mind. We just are not fond of ultimatums. Very few of us are going to spring up with
an engagement ring because you told us to deliver
or hit the road. And if you succeed in pressuring
us into making a commitment, we'll find ourselves
questioning our motives somewhere down the
road. And that is not an encouraging omen for either of us.

The good news is that there are moments in a
man's life, turning points if you will, when he re-
alizes he wants to be married. For the perpetual
bachelor, it might be the last meaningless date with
someone he meets at a bar or a party. We once
again find ourselves making small talk over drinks
or forcing laughter over cheap pasta and house
wine. And then the inevitable stroll back to her
place or ours. The mumbled faux affections, the
scattered clothes, and the embarrassed fumbling
with the blue-sheathed condom as we make love
(hardly the appropriate words) to someone we
barely know and can hardly differentiate from the
last one hundred dates. We wake up the next
morning, look at this naked stranger, and think:
"Gee. There's got to be more than this!"

Every man goes through this epiphany eventually. Something in our psyche changes. It might
not happen overnight. But we start to view our
dating habits in a different light. The whole conquest theory flies out the window. We stop going
on dates with women whom we only want to go to
bed with. Even the ones with the great bodies. And

when we do meet someone who seems extra special, we become more timid in our advances. Kim, a New Orleans businesswoman, recalls how "slow" her husband Phil was in their early dating days. She still teases him mercilessly about the fact that he did not kiss her goodnight on the first date. And they did not start having sex for almost two months.

Phil takes Kim's teasing good-naturedly, because he knew that in Kim, he had met the woman who would be his match. And the last thing he wanted to do was treat her in the same way he had treated a thousand and one previous dates. It's not that he was mean or ill-mannered to the others, but he wanted Kim to be special. She thought he was slow. He thought she was incredible. And he made every moment of their relationship a new and unique one, right up to and including flashing his marriage proposal on the scoreboard of the Superdome at a Saints game.

For the man who has been dating a woman for a very long time, or living with his girlfriend, the "moment" may come from a seemingly mundane event or chore. Buying a matching set of iced tea glasses for summer. Or shopping together for a new car. Baby-sitting for a friend's kids, or taking your parents out to dinner. Some men get hit over the head in love and propose in a lightning heartbeat. Others are the more gradual type, and it is the comfort of the situation that inspires a man to spring the question. The fact is, if our relationship is rock solid and we find ourselves sharing in more and more of life's daily pleasures, then we are eventually going to work up the nerve to propose.

And the "moment" is no less special to us. It just might take a little longer coming.

When Romance Flies

The first time he ever laid eyes on you, it was as if he had been glued to the spot. Maybe you were talking to another guy at a party, or standing alone reading your paper on the subway, or sitting cross-legged on the office floor going through a stack of files. Can you remember what he looked like mouth agape, not saying a word? He knew you were the one, but damn if he had a clue how he was going to get anywhere. And so began the courtship. He was stunned that you weren't totally wrapped up with another guy, and thrilled that you said yes to dinner. He remembers your amazing first date, and will never forget the softness of your lips and the sweet scent still on his clothes as he walked away after saying goodnight, wondering how he could speed up the clock until the next time he saw you.

He still gets a catch in the throat when he thinks of the first time he kissed your naked breast, the sound of your clothes falling softly to the floor, the light shining gently through your bedroom window as you made love for the very first time. Those memories are painted in his heart, and a thousand nights on he can still evoke that feeling as he holds you in his arms.

So what was he looking for when he found you? That's impossible to answer. Life is just not that predictable. He'll say that he wants someone to swill beers and bellow at a ball game with him, but he also wants to melt with her over a romantic dinner in a tiny cafe. He'll tell you he wants a woman happy to spend Friday night curled up in her favorite chair reading a book. But he'll drool with delight when you put on a drop-dead sexy dress and take him dancing until dawn. He wants a girlfriend who reaches out with one arm in her sleep just to feel him there, as well as a woman who makes wild love to him in the middle of the living room floor—and he wants them both to be you. A tough order perhaps. But that's where fate steps in.

Marshall and Liza met while working together at a magazine in New York City. For a town of nine million, New York may well be the loneliest place on earth if you are trying to go it alone. Liza, just coming off her umpteenth failed relationship with a noncommittal creep, was absolutely ready to swear off dating. Tom Cruise could have come knocking at her door and she would have told him to take a hike. Marshall was as jaded, if not more so, with what he perceived as "impossible" New York City women. To him, they all seemed to be big-game hunting for doctors, lawyers, bankers, or anyone else who could offer a lifetime guarantee of professional and financial stability. The women he dated wanted Porsches, beach houses, ski houses, and a Fifth Avenue duplex. Not to mention sex twice a day, with a three-orgasm clause written into a six-figure prenuptial agreement. For Marshall, dating had become more of a job than a pleasure.

Was his attraction to Liza instantaneous? Not exactly. He thought she was kind of pretty. And very friendly. And always out on a date! As a matter of fact, their friendship began when he started to rib her about the number of suitors she had. And so, Liza began to confide in Marshall about all the lovely habits of the men she dated. The clothes they wore, the restaurants they dragged her to, the fumbled passes, and the selfish expectations. The more jerks Liza dated, the more Marshall realized how difficult it was to be a single woman in New York City. He also realized how fond of Liza he was growing.

For about two months, Liza and Marshall traded horror stories about their social lives. They grew to know each other and laugh at each other, all in a safe environment where there was no risk of rejection. Finally, a Friday night rolled around when Liza did not have a date and Marshall had just been blown off by a woman he had met at the health club. So they decided to go home from work, change, and meet up for a few beers and a burger later on that evening. Very casual . . . No threat at all.

Marshall had never seen Liza outside of work or in casual clothes before. So when she walked into the downtown tavern where he sat at the bar waiting, he didn't recognize her immediately. Besides, he was busy having his heart turned upside down by a gal wearing blue jeans, a cotton tee, hair in a ponytail, and no makeup. She had on canvas tennis shoes, a cute ball cap, and had a spring to her step that left him thunderstruck. So much so that it took him a moment to realize that the woman who had caught his eye *was Liza.* She looked so different from work that it truly was like meeting her for the very first time.

Marshall and Liza knocked back some beers and burgers. They went to a piano bar and sang old show tunes with the locals until three-thirty in the morning. They wandered over to the all-night diner and shared a greasy souvlaki sandwich. And as they walked back to Liza's apartment, they realized their jaws were sore from smiling all evening.

Liza invited Marshall up for a cup of coffee. It was almost five in the morning. And no, sorry to disappoint, but this story does not end with them making passionate love as the sun came up over Manhattan. They talked. And talked some more.

Their "moment" came during a Jackson Browne song that they had both loved during their college days. Well, first kisses, right? Good times. Marshall and Liza made out until their lips were tingling and Liza's face was beard-burned. If you ask Marshall today, he can still tell you which line of the song was playing when they first kissed, and he'll describe the streets as he walked home alone at dawn, still humming that song. He remembers the color of the sky and the name of the dog who was out for a walk in front of his apartment building (Chloe). And he especially remembers the answering machine message that was waiting for him when he walked into his apartment. It was from Liza, and she said: "Hi. It's me. I'm lying here in bed and my face is all red and scratchy from your beard. I just wanted you to know . . . You're still here with me . . ." Click! We should all fall in love so happily.

There comes a day in a man's life when dating becomes a chore and what we want more than anything is a companion. A girlfriend whom we can shower with attention. Someone who laughs at our jokes and likes our ripped jeans and can put up with our friends. A woman who makes us think about kids and dinner parties, of rides in the country with the windows open and our fingers lightly touching as we sing old songs and wind down a road we've never traveled before.

When that day arrives, we want a lover who sends a shiver down our spines—a partner who can balance a checkbook, whip up a good marinade, and change a tire. But more than anything, we want a woman who is our best friend. For the good times. For the bad times. And especially, for the long run.

PART TWO

THE LONG RUN

CHAPTER 6:

In Love with the 90s Career Woman

Larry and Tina met in business school, married a year later, landed jobs on the West Coast, and set off for San Diego with a car full of junk and a future full of dreams. While Tina settled into a consulting job with a local think tank and felt right at home, Larry was not so lucky. He had taken a position with a San Diego bank. Talk about the wrong job for the wrong guy!

According to Tina, the Larry she fell in love with was a serious student with a flair for the ridiculous. He played in a rock and roll band, dabbled in something he called modern art, and served as a big brother in the local community. Now he spent his days in a suit and tie, watching the clock and wondering why anyone would choose to do something as stupendously meaningless as crunching numbers for the rest of his life. Arguably, he should never have gone to business school in the first place, but that is an expensive mistake to atone for when you have two years of student loans to worry about. So, Larry punched the clock and Tina watched his spirit ebb, until she knew it was time to take action.

She snatched him from the office one sunny afternoon and dragged him to a lovely spot overlooking the Pacific in La Jolla. Tina spread out a blanket, served a gourmet lunch, and engaged him in a heart-to-heart about his career choice and how unsatisfied he seemed. She reminded Larry that having an MBA didn't sentence him to a lifetime in a suit and tie, and mentioned several friends who had used their degrees to land jobs far from the staid world of banking. Why not look for something else? Tina urged. Her salary could support the two of them for several months while he sought out a more appropriate job.

This was a pep talk Larry desperately needed. And it was so effective that after a two-hour nap in the California sunshine, Larry went back to his office, turned in his resignation, and packed his briefcase. Two soul-searching months later he took a development job at a major university.

In the not-so-distant past, few wives were inclined or in a position to carry the ball financially while their husbands searched for more meaningful career paths. Few men could have tolerated that much help in an area that had long been considered their domain. But Larry and Tina are a thoroughly modern nineties couple who share equally in every decision they make. Tina is an educated and highly independent woman with a successful career. Larry respects and loves her as both a bright, competent professional *and* a terrific mate. And he is not alone.

Today, men have come to appreciate, even prefer, career women as lifetime partners. This doesn't mean that we expect them to be the sole breadwinner, fast-tracking bank vice president, and primary caretaker of our children while we polish our putting skills on the front nine. But we do want to settle down with a woman who is willing to negotiate a new professional landscape with us as well as share responsibility in everything from raising a family to stealing away for an occasional week off at the shore.

We've Come a Long Way, Baby

To some, Tina's offer to financially support Larry's career change might seem a huge sacrifice. To Tina it was the only thing to do. She knew Larry wasn't cut out to be one of the "suits" when she married him. And on their wedding day, they both had promised to stand by each other through various ups and downs. Traditionally, that has meant for richer or poorer and through sickness or in health. But today's vows probably should be updated to include "in employment and in transition," because most couples will face that kind of hardship sooner or later.

In Brad and Linda's case, it was sooner. They moved in together in New York City after dating for a year and were immediately influenced by New York's own peculiar effect on relationships. Since living there is so expensive, most matters pale in comparison to the question, "How in God's name are we going to make rent?"

Brad was struggling along as a junior copywriter, enjoying the job despite its long hours. And he maintained a positive attitude about the salary, even though, as in most entry-level creative positions, it was dirt. Since he aspired to run his own agency someday, the learning and networking opportunities outweighed the fact that he couldn't afford much more than macaroni and cheese with his current pay. Linda, on the other hand, was pulling down a decent salary as an account executive for an entertainment public relations firm. Between the two of them, they were more or less getting by.

Unfortunately, while Brad was making slave wages in a fun position with a potential future payoff, Linda was toting the bulk of their financial load by slaving away in a job she hated. Her boss was a fool and her clients self-absorbed celebrities whose shows pretty much filled out the spectrum of bad late-night television. Her true aspirations lay in nonprofit work. If money were no object, she would have happily been handing out bread at the local soup kitchen or working with a coalition for the homeless. But money did matter and one of life's great inequities is that a job touting the wonders of pay-per-view pro wrestling pays a lot more than a position with a major charity. So, when Linda happened upon a golden job opportunity working for a prestigious nonprofit, she had to approach Brad with the first major dilemma of their relationship: Does she take a $12,000-a-year pay cut to accept a stimulating job in the field of her dreams or turn it down to continue being the breadwinner, until Brad's salary gets up to speed?

Linda did not have to worry. This was a no-brainer for Brad. He insisted that she take the job at the nonprofit, despite the hefty pay cut. He seized the moment to approach his boss and cajole something of a promotion and a pay raise out of him. In addition, to help offset their reduced income, Brad returned to an old college vocation—deejaying at parties on weekends for extra cash. Even so, Brad and Linda struggled for quite a while. They cooked at home most nights. Fresh pasta from the gourmet store was replaced by three-for-a-dollar boxes of generic-brand spaghetti. Friday nights out at the movies (for twenty bucks minimum) became Friday nights in with rented videos and microwave popcorn. And the only weekends they managed to get out of town were the ones when a friend or a relative offered a free bed to stay in—regardless of where that might be. (One learns to love the Catskills when there's not a spare room to be found near the shore.) Brad and Linda soon adjusted to the slightly modified early life plan that they had to follow until their combined salaries climbed back up to (and eventually beyond) their previous level. The scrimping was worth it, they agreed, to both be working in careers that they loved and believed in.

Linda's role in their relationship is indicative of exactly where today's career woman has come. She is an equal partner, and accepted as such by any man worth his Barney's suit. Or hardhat. Or saddle and boots. The Ward and June Cleaver notion that the man works while the apron-wearing "little lady" stays home and waits for her hubby to return from the office is dead. We are living in a new age and a new economy. Everything our parents had, and that we may well aspire to, costs significantly more today than anyone ever imagined. Chances are that both of us will *have* to work full time to pay the mortgage, own two cars, and keep whole-wheat pesto ravioli in the fridge.

This doesn't exactly come as a surprise to today's men. We knew when we were in college with you, sweating out all-nighters and exams and job interviews, that we'd both be entering the real world on the run and as equals. There still might be some men out there who sport the old-fashioned notion of marrying a woman to iron their shirts, bear their children, and manage the carpool. No doubt, there also are women who would happily chuck their jobs to stay home and run a household. That's their prerogative. But on the whole, men and women begin new relationships as counterparts in the workplace. And that sense of equality, by necessity, carries over into our personal lives. It's as if we're now going "dutch" on a whole lot more than a date. Unless one of us was born with a huge trust fund or recently inherited a small fortune, we'll both be entering the rat race each morning and hopefully coming home to a partner who will share in making every aspect of life bearable.

Today, the single-income household has become a relic of the past. Couples work, earn, suffer, worry over money matters, and share in the fiscal responsibility *together*. So much so that work and work-related problems can control our lives. They're less likely to, though, if we coordinate our professional goals and work towards a common end, plotting our career paths as fastidiously as we planned the menu for our weddings.

Whose Career First?

Stan and Missy, married almost three years, have each seen their careers take unexpected twists and turns. In many ways, the decisions they have made and where those decisions led them are representative of many couples trying to make ends meet in today's challenging economy.

Their courtship began in southern California, where Missy was working her way up the corporate ladder in a marketing job with a major women's products company. Stan, a former office machine salesman from Cleveland, had chucked it all to make a go of it in L.A.'s more relaxed atmosphere. He found employment as a groundskeeper for an elite gardening agency in Beverly Hills, discovered that he thoroughly enjoyed the work, and started to dream about establishing his own landscape architecture business. For the first six months of their relationship, Missy donned a business suit to her office while Stan worked bare-chested in the outdoors six days a week—and had the tan to prove it. When they became engaged, Missy was making almost double Stan's salary.

Soon after the wedding, though, life took a series of unexpected hairpin turns. Missy's seemingly stable company went Chapter 11 and snapped her burgeoning corporate career to freeze-frame. Then, just as Missy was settling in for what would turn out to be a lengthy job hunt, Stan's employer decided that he'd had enough of L.A., and moved his business up the coast to Santa Barbara. This left Stan to wear out shoe leather on the unemployment lines along with his new bride.

Missy kept hearing that she would have to return to school and earn her MBA if she was going to continue to climb the corporate ladder. Stan was no more encouraged by his attempts to land freelance landscaping work. Since there were already more than enough gardeners in Los Angeles, he kept coming up empty-handed. So, with their joint savings evaporating and no prospects, Missy and Stan took stock and devised an entirely new plan of action.

Missy applied to and was accepted for a one-year accelerated MBA program at Northwestern University in Chicago. She was eligible for a small amount of financial aid, but not nearly enough to put her through school, much less support two people. So she and Stan struck a deal. While she was doing her year of studies, he would find a job—the best-paying job he could turn up—to cover their expenses. After graduating with a degree that almost certainly assured her of a decent-paying position, Missy would assume the financial load and Stan could spend the next year pursuing any endeavor he desired.

With this compromise reached, they packed the U-Haul and shipped off to Evanston, Illinois, where Missy studied for twenty hours a day and Stan became a maitre d' at a well-known Chicago restaurant. They struggled, scrimped, and scraped by, testing their financial and romantic endurance. (After a year of easygoing living in the sunny climes of L.A., winter on Lake Michigan would test anyone's mettle.) They survived, though, and a month after earning her degree, Missy had job offers in several major U.S. cities. When she accepted a marketing position with a corporation in Kansas

City, Stan seated his last diners at the Chicago restaurant and loaded up the U-Haul for the second time in ten months. Upon their arrival, Stan discovered a large, untapped market for an experienced landscaper. With the superior training he'd received while manicuring lawns in Beverly Hills, he had little trouble establishing a client base. Just eighteen months after teetering on the brink of financial ruin in Los Angeles, Missy was back on track with a strong and secure company, Stan had his own business, and they were buying their first home in Kansas City. Having played adversity as well as a couple could, they ended up with a winning hand.

Contrary to popular belief, when it comes to supporting a family, men are not always as bullheaded as you might think. Most of us don't want to go it alone or as the sole partner who shoulders the entire burden of responsibility by ourselves. We may have taken the lead in picking the movie or restaurant on our first few dates, but that does not mean we are going to decide where we grow old together. We want your input.

In today's work force, depending on our individual career choices, there's a good chance you'll earn as much, if not more, than we do. Consequently, we need to know where your professional dreams and ambitions lie, even as we plot our own courses. You might be a lawyer, doctor, or a banker, and we might have to bend to accommodate your high-paying job. Or we might use our earning power to let you take advantage of an opportunity that you otherwise might not have been able to consider. Or vice versa. For instance, when Gary, a city planner and talented jazz guitarist,

married Sarah, a handsomely paid pediatrician,
her six-figure salary afforded him the luxury of
choice. He could stick with his professional vocation or follow his heart and try to make a living as
a session guitarist. As it turned out, he managed to
do both, and he and Sarah split their financial responsibilities right down the middle. But before he
ever earned a nickel playing his guitar, Sarah made
it clear that she wanted him to pursue whichever
path made him happy. They planned out their financial future, together, and both were fortunate to
find satisfaction in their careers.

By the time you reach your late twenties and
early thirties, you probably will have carved out a
professional niche for yourself, and if you've remained single for most of that time, you've probably grown accustomed to supporting yourself. You
have paid off student loans, purchased at least one
car, and maybe even bought your first apartment
or home. You don't need someone to step into
your life romantically and then tell you what to do
with your money or your career. And most men
don't want to. We'd rather meld into an equal partnership and jointly chart out our separate paths.

Let's assume for a moment that money is not an
issue. You and your mate both have stable jobs
with decent salaries and a promising future. Could
work still shake up your household? You bet. Just
ask Bill, a Houston real estate broker. One week after he moved in with his girlfriend, Anne, a man-
agement consultant, she accepted a six-month
assignment in Singapore. It was a prestigious post-
ing and she assumed that Bill would be support-
ive, not to mention accommodating. But he was
not. The way he saw it, they hadn't even unpacked

their CDs yet and suddenly they were facing an eight-thousand-mile separation. What's more, she had accepted the position without consulting him. If she had, the prospect of having an absentee girlfriend still might not have thrilled Bill, but at least he would have known that Anne cared enough about him to include him in the decision-making process. Feeling as if he came third on Anne's list of priorities (after career and travel), Bill engaged her in a brief and ugly battle that ended with them splitting up.

When a professional move has the potential to impact a relationship, ask yourself how you'd like your significant other to deal with it. Chances are that you *wouldn't* want to hear: "Hi honey, I'm home. Got some good news and some bad news. You know how much you like sushi? Well, the good news is you're going to be eating a lot of it. The bad news is . . ."

You and your guy owe it to each other to make these decisions together. If it's our career dilemma, you can be as strong, opinionated, and even argumentative as the situation seems to warrant. In fact, we want you to be because we don't want to make a rotten decision—or have to live it down—alone.

Of course, not all career-related crises are as clear-cut as Bill and Anne's. Andy and Maureen, wed eight years, were both highly paid lawyers in separate Boston firms. Maureen made partner first and was well on her way to a financial windfall. Throughout the course of their marriage, she had always assumed that Andy was aiming for partner, too, and together they would ride off into the sunset with a few million dollars tucked into their saddlebags. However, when partnership seemed to be passing Andy by, Maureen began to wonder whether he was truly motivated to reach the top in their fiercely competitive field. Finally, she came right out and asked him if something was wrong.

As it turned out, Andy was thoroughly disenchanted with the law and had basically lost interest in his job. Unbeknownst to his wife, he had sent away for dozens of applications to grad schools that offered teaching degrees. What's more, in his spare time he had penciled six hundred pages of a novel that he kept under lock and key in the top drawer of his desk. Granted, he had not filled out any of the applications, and the pages of the novel were growing dry and brittle from being locked up for so long. But still, they were there, a manifestation of Andy's unhappiness with his career.

Maureen was astounded. She never had a clue. And if she had not asked, she may never have known. Andy would have continued stockpiling grad school applications, and their marriage would have gone on under this subterfuge, probably until they retired. But then, Maureen had a few unspoken desires up her sleeve as well. She also was anxious to get out of corporate law (though she hadn't planned to quite as soon). Her goal was to switch her focus to environmental law and hopefully move out of the city to a smaller New England town where she would eventually have kids and raise them while working a job with more tolerable hours.

Andy and Maureen's is a story about communication. Or more precisely, the lack thereof. Andy toiled in quiet misery, never confiding his doubts about the direction his career was headed. Maureen never voiced her long-term goals either, leaving Andy in the dark about her true wishes and dreams. These two corporate attorneys were fortunate to discover that their true passions and interests lay far beyond the sterile walls of a Boston law firm, and change was only possible when they finally started talking to each other.

How the women in our lives feel about *their* work is a matter of great importance to us. Please, don't keep us in the dark when it comes to discussing your professional life. We want to know if you are happy. We need to know if you are miserable. It kills us to have to guess what's going on in your mind. If you leave it up to us, we'll surely miss some of the warning signs, including obvious ones such as coming home from work in a bad mood every day for a month. We'll think, "Well, lots of people come home from work in a bad mood. That's why we have jobs. To get beaten up, emotionally bruised, or underpaid, and come home from work in a bad mood." How were we supposed to know that this bad mood was different, and that you really were sick of being personnel director for the Glop Corporation?

Unless you tell us, we'll never know that you wish you could finish your paramedic training and join the rescue squad, or try your hand at catering. Even if your dreams are thoroughly unrealistic and don't fit easily into our career paths, we'd still rather know what you're thinking. We're not easily shocked (although telling us you plan to give up your dental practice to become a topless dancer might do it).

We want to work in harmony with you, especial-

ly when a change is in the offing. So, if you are se-
cretly in training for the next Iditarod Race, give us
a hint. Yes, we might laugh at you—for an instant.
But we also might be rather impressed. And we
might turn around and surprise you by confessing
our secret desire to buy a tuna fishing boat in
Alaska and escape the city grind. Bingo! We can
follow our dreams together.

A basic premise applies: Relationships suffer
when one or both of us are miserable at work but
unable or unwilling to say so. We get into a rut
and start to accept that miserable is the way life is
going to be. This is seriously unhealthy behavior.
Unless we get work problems out into the open,
our romance may go into a tailspin. The same
holds true in other areas of our relationship where
change has the potential to be traumatic—or a real
life boost.

Raising the Kids

Crying. Screaming. Burping. Wet clothes. Mess
everywhere. You thought it was tough being
around us at the sports bar? Wait until you have
some real kids. Parenthood is one of the few things
that can get men to finally go up on the roof and
clean out the gutters. Almost anything is more desirable than changing a diaper on a ninety-eight-
degree summer day. Unfortunately, since we have
accepted the role as equals in our relationship, we
must come to terms with that and other less delec-
table aspects of raising our progeny.

You see, we didn't really know what we were
getting into. We imagined taking adorable snap-
shots of newborns and coaching the Little League

team—without fully appreciating the gap in between. We sort of assumed that those eight years would pass without incident or disruption to our normal lives. Still, even those of us not yet blessed with wife or child have learned that the issue of bringing up the young ones is touchy and best dealt with far in advance of wallpapering the new baby's room.

Many of us *do* want to have children—and not just to coach their sports teams or see their college stickers on the back of the station wagon. So how do we make this monumental decision to pass on the family name? Preferably not by accident. And usually *after* we're married.

Of course, some men absolutely do *not* want kids. They are the worst possible match for women who are driven by their maternal instincts. Since you don't want to discover on your honeymoon that your husband is steadfastly opposed to the idea of having a family, you should seriously consider discussing the matter prior to the eve of your wedding and hopefully before you become engaged.

There are good ways and not so good ways to do that. Here's one way *not* to. Over dinner on your third date, ask: "Mel, do you want to have kids someday?" That's just a little too blunt and a little too soon. You might as well ask how we feel about dentures and retirement plans. We're still trying to figure out if that's a French lace bra you're wearing underneath your blouse! Having children is a wonderful thing, but thinking about them is not exactly an aphrodisiac. We're just getting to know you. Let us hone the fine art of bring-

ing you to an orgasm or two before we consider
the prospect of producing a family.

As the relationship grows, however, you will
want to subtly probe for a man's parenting potential. Try taking him to visit a friend or relative who
has children. Young children. In diapers. Who
scream a lot. See how he responds. If he snaps and
growls like a pit bull, you might want to explore
this issue a bit further. Likewise, if he sneaks out of
your twin nieces' birthday party and spends the
entire afternoon in a back bedroom swilling beer
and watching the ball game, the ride home might
be a good time to ask if there is a problem.

Men tend to be very straightforward on this subject. We do not consider children a laughing matter. There was a time when "safe sex" mainly
meant wearing a condom so that we would not accidentally get you pregnant. We took this responsibility seriously, and our attitude hasn't changed. A
man who knows he never wants to be a father will
tell you. There is no faking it.

If you are at a point in your relationship where
you are asking, and he is clearly not the daddy
type, be prepared for the consequences. The "she
wants kids and he doesn't" crossroad is often the
stop where he gets off. In the long run, parting
company will be the best thing for both of you, because he doesn't want to string you along, nor do
you want to try to have a family with a man who
does not want one.

There's really no compromise solution. We are
either going to commit our hearts, minds, and lives
to raising our babies or we aren't. As soon as you
suspect that you are dating a man who has no interest in being a father to the children you defi-

nitely want, you are well advised to accept that and move on.

Now, suppose that we both do share in the desire to raise a family together. Someday. Beyond the obvious issue of *which* day, there are many factors to consider. Finances, for instance.

As their second anniversary approached, Cynthia was holding an average job with a less-than-average salary in the newspaper business, and Mark worked at a soft-drink company. They lived in a pricey one-bedroom apartment in a newly renovated section of Baltimore. It suited their lifestyle perfectly. They had intimate dinner parties with their downtown friends and were a five-minute walk from the ballpark at Camden Yards. There was only one drawback: The high cost of city living ate up every cent they earned. If they were going to start a family—which they both wanted to do—they had to start saving money. And if they were going to save money, something had to change.

The answer to their problems? Move to the Maryland countryside where their combined income would have a lot more clout. They made a bold decision to do that and not only reduced their overhead significantly, but also were able to increase their living space, buy a decent car, and put money away for the eventual new arrival. Although they sometimes missed their old lifestyle and occasionally wished they could be more spontaneous about expanding their family, their move and advance planning was a compromise they both readily accepted.

Money isn't the only deciding factor in having children, of course. Take Amanda and Ian for ex-

ample. They had been married five years and were
living in San Francisco where Amanda was a successful film editor. Ian, a perpetual student (with a
substantial trust fund), was studying astrophysics
with a vague notion of seeking an advanced degree so that he might someday get on board a
space shuttle flight. While he pursued this latest in
a long line of quests for a vocation that reflected
his true self, Amanda thought about babies. As she
neared thirty, her mind was on motherhood more
than movies. But how could she justify having a
child when she was already living with one?

It wasn't that their marriage was bad. It was just
that Ian acted as if he was still a 22-year-old without
a care in the world. He got caught up in conversations with people he ran into on the way to the
pharmacy and returned hours later without the item
he went out to purchase. When he was lost in
thought or absorbed by a "Nova" program on PBS,
he tuned out everything including the smell of food
burning on the stove. Could he be trusted to tend to
an infant or keep a toddler from getting into trouble
or even remember that a child was asleep upstairs?
If not, would Amanda have to assume all the responsibility for raising their offspring (along with
working outside the home)? Was she willing to do
that? Did Ian really want kids at all?

"Eventually," had been Ian's reply in the past, but
Amanda needed a more specific answer now. She
sat Ian down and explained her point of view. She
listened to his reservations about becoming a father
before he'd fully explored who he was as a person.
And, finally, together they set some deadlines for
how long they would wait before they started trying
to have kids.

Ian's delay in becoming a dad is not uncommon. Many men think of fatherhood in much the same way they thought about marriage. They equate it with the end of an era and the beginning of irreversible changes in their lifestyle. Of course, a woman's lifestyle is going to change too. Your role in bringing a child into the world is both emotional and physical. We cannot begin to know what it feels like to be pregnant nor imagine what maternal instinct is. We have it easy, you say. Lots of sex until you break the news, then nine months of waiting to hand out big fat cigars while you lie dopey-eyed and exhausted in the recovery room.

Arguably, we do have it easier. But talk to a dozen men and you will find that there are some pretty complicated emotions at work for us too. We are afraid of growing older. We shudder at the prospect of turning into *our* fathers. And the responsibility involved in raising a child seems so enormous, especially when we know we've had exactly zero training for it.

So please, when you broach the subject of having a child, don't underestimate the emotional commitment your mate may feel he's being asked to make. He's not just spewing flowery sentiments when he says he wants to be there with you through the entire process. And while he isn't lugging around twenty-five additional pounds or watching his feet swell up larger than basketballs, he can empathize, and often will do anything for you if you'll let him share in the experience. Some dads are in the delivery room videotaping the birth. Others are in the waiting room gnawing their fingernails down to the quick, awaiting word from the doctor. Either way, this is their baby too.

As prospective fathers, we want to help design the nursery, pick wonderful names for the grandparents to criticize, and be as much a part of the planning for the blessed event as we can. After all, like you, we are going to be living with our "decision" for at least the next eighteen years of our lives.

Making the Home-Office Work

Nancy, a Wall Street bond trader, managed to swing her high-flying career and pregnancy without so much as a pause. She worked right up until the day she went into labor, and she had her firm provide her with a Quotron and a fax machine in the hospital room. I'll never know if she actually transacted any deals as her firstborn, Peter, came down the birth canal, but she was back on the phones within twelve hours of delivery. Maybe this is admirable. Maybe this is true commitment to a career. Or perhaps it is just over-the-top obsessiveness about a fast-track job. But with today's advanced home-office technology, even less driven professionals can stay at home with a newborn infant without giving up (or losing time on) their job. We can conference call, fax, and link our computers from any nursery in the world. And if working from home is not possible, on-site childcare may be. Many companies have day-care centers on the premises so that parents can stay close to their children *and* on top of their jobs.

Because of this newfound freedom to combine our work and home lives, there are new matters couples need to talk over before their first child is born. If you are a career woman, do you want to take a long leave of absence after having a baby? Will your company and financial circumstances allow this? And if you are planning to return to the work force quickly (or anytime in the foreseeable future), who is going to take care of the baby when you do? There are men who are up to that task and would love to stay home. There also are men who expect you to dump your career aspirations the day a child is born, as well as men who are uncertain and saying to themselves, "If my wife has a higher-paying job than I do, maybe I *should* play 'Mr. Mom' for a while and let her continue to be the numero uno breadwinner." These are not lightweight issues, and they should not be left to fate.

Adam, a mortgage loan officer and his wife Bobbi, a graphic artist, live in a Denver suburb with their two young sons, Thomas and Michael. Before they started their family, Adam and Bobbi both held office jobs in their respective fields. Bobbi was the first to switch to a home career. Right after Thomas was born, she signed a lucrative contract to do freelance design work for her previous employer, and quickly began attracting other clients as well. They were happy to use her services on a project basis and save the money they would have spent on benefits for a full-time employee.

Adam was proud of his wife's success, but also jealous of her home-office set-up. Here she was simultaneously experiencing the joys of raising their firstborn and making a great income working out of their basement. There was no commute. No aggravating office politics to deal with on a daily basis. She didn't have to deal with any of the less appealing aspects of working full time in an office full of people. And so, when their second child was born, Adam followed Bobbi's lead, and found a position that required more field work and less office time. When he wasn't on the road or with clients, he was home having lunch with Bobbi and the boys, faxing documents from the basement office, or staying in touch with his clients by beeper while teaching Thomas how to swim at the neighborhood pool.

The notion of keeping our jobs while staying home, taking care of the baby, and maybe even catching Wimbledon live from England during the day can be rather appealing. The question men like Adam are asking is: "Why should women have all the fun?" Of course, we know that raising a child isn't all fun and games, but still, some of us want to stay home to do it. At the very least, we'd like to forge career paths that allow us to play a much larger part in our kids' upbringing than some of our own fathers did.

Many of us have childhood memories of watching other kids tossing a ball with their fathers or other dads watering the lawn at the end of the day, while *our* dads worked late (and came home too tired or wired to pay much attention to us). Those are not happy memories. And most of us would prefer not to be that kind of absentee father to our children. Maybe our dads couldn't pick us up at day camp, or go to PTA meetings, or be "den mother" on camping trips, but we can—and want to.

Rusty and Deirdre went the traditional route when their two children, Gail and Paul, were born. Deirdre gave up her accounting job to stay home with the kids while Rusty continued working as a

TV commercial producer. For more than a decade, this situation seemed to suit them both. But Deirdre's thinking changed when Gail reached high-school age and was old enough to care for her brother after school. Although Deirdre still had plenty of child-rearing responsibilities, the load was lighter than it had been when the kids were younger, and she had begun to miss the workplace. She told Rusty she wanted to go back to work, and rather than arguing against it as impractical, he was more than happy to have Deirdre rejoin the corporate world. In fact, he saw it as a grand opportunity to leave his full-time job, offer his producing services on a freelance basis, and become more involved in parenting.

When Deirdre and Rusty switched roles, everyone won. Deirdre got to return to the work force in a career she had long ago enjoyed. Rusty escaped the nine-to-five grind. And their children benefitted from their dad's daily presence, guidance, and encouragement as they grew into young adults.

Ideally, in the nineties and beyond, raising a family will be a team effort with men and women making decisions about managing their professional and family lives. If we've lived on a joint income for five years prior to the birth of our first child and now one of us is going to stay home with the baby, we have to decide which one of us it will be. If both of us are going to continue on in our careers, we both need a say in decisions about child care. And if you're thinking of quitting your job to bear and raise a dozen children, definitely clue us in so we can decide how many jobs *we'll* have to work to pay for all their braces and piano lessons.

Clearly, there are lots of options open to us, and couples need to talk about them. This does not mean that the day you announce you are pregnant, we'll start a knockdown, drag-out battle over who gets to stay home with the kids. But we do want to know that there will be some give and take when it comes to structuring the home in which we'll raise our children.

But what happens when the kids go off to college, or to distant cities in pursuit of exciting job offers? Does this mean the challenging times are over? Believe me, two-career couples will still have plenty to talk about when that day arrives.

Victor and Sandi lived in Texas where Sandi was the vice president of a small oil company and Victor was a successful building contractor. They had been married twenty-plus years when Victor announced that it was time for a change. It turned out, he had long harbored dreams of running a restaurant, and now that their only child was grown up and married, he felt safe in approaching Sandi with this starry-eyed notion. Much to his surprise, she confessed to being tired of living in Texas. She wanted to wake up smelling an ocean breeze, and she was more than willing to blow a substantial chunk of their savings on buying into a restaurant for Victor—if it was in a town of her choosing. With this bargain struck, soon Victor was frying fish at a seaside shanty he opened on the Oregon coast, and Sandi was senior vice president of a shipping concern in Portland.

The Politics of Sacrifice

Sharing responsibilities in these difficult economic times goes beyond simply splitting the bills. You might be half of a two-career couple because you both have to work to make ends meet. But neither of you has to be miserable in your job. In times of change, you and your partner can cover each other financially. And when kids come along, you can bend the traditional roles to maintain both of your careers.

The American dream used to be own a house, have three kids, and retire early. Today we're forced to operate on a modified plan: own a house (preferably without taking out a second or third mortgage), have a child or two (if you can afford to and your company offers good child-care benefits and maternity leave), and forget about early retirement. Just hope you've wisely invested what little you can scrape together so your kids have a prayer of going to college.

What does a man want from his partner under those circumstances? Being the heir to a fortune would be a plus. Chairman of the board of a major company also has its merits. But realistically speaking, we want and need someone who will share the responsibility in the hard times as well as the good. And this has a lot less to do with hard cash dollars than it does with planning for our future together.

DeeDee and Mark are a perfect example of a couple who realistically set themselves up for a long and comfortable life together, beginning with their engagement. They met at the shore—Amagansett, Long Island, to be exact. Their romance was conducted amidst the dunes. The beach was in their blood, and they both longed to own a cottage there one day. Consequently, when DeeDee's parents offered to throw a lavish country club "do" in honor of her nuptials, Mark had an unorthodox suggestion. He knew that the cost of a wedding today was only slightly less than his parents' generation paid for their first houses. And it occurred to him that instead of accepting DeeDee's parents' generous offer for a lavish reception, they might ask for a comparable sum to be used as a down payment on their beach cottage and then host a smaller, more intimate wedding reception themselves.

While some might consider this a rather cheeky proposal, DeeDee's father agreed with Mark's logic, applauded him for his practicality, and wrote out a check. Three months after holding a small, lovely wedding reception at an out-of-the-way restaurant with only family and a group of their closest friends in attendance, Mark and DeeDee found a "fix-it-up" cottage in a quaint village less than a mile from the sea. They spent the winter painting, building, mending, decorating, and handling every last detail themselves. Today, they rent out the cottage for half the summer to recoup their entire mortgage, and then in August, when all of New York would kill for a country place with a yard and a deck one mile from the beach, they spend the whole month on holiday, relaxing, bicycling, playing tennis, and entertaining their best friends and family. What did they sacrifice for this luxury? One night of Beluga caviar and Dom Perignon, and a lot of rich relatives yawning through another society wedding. All in all, it was an exciting and novel way to start their marriage.

CHAPTER 7:

Keeping Him Faithful

Walter, a 35-year-old computer salesman for a large national company, has been married ten years and lives with his wife Helen, a house mom, and their three children in a lovely four-bedroom home in the Houston suburbs. Walter's income is handsome, his wife smart and pretty, and his kids happy and healthy. He has a successful marriage and a good life, by almost anyone's standards including his own.

So, what happened when he was invited to a three-day convention in San Diego? He turned around and had an affair. Totally out of the blue and for the first time, he cheated on Helen and risked his entire family life for what might seem a very small payoff: sex with a woman who wasn't his wife. Why did Walter do it? Why do other seemingly happy husbands do it? What strange evil lurks in the minds of men that compels them to risk everything for largely meaningless, immediate gratification?

The woman Walter slept with (I'll call her Lindsay), was twenty-four years old, attractive,

single, and from Dayton, Ohio. Like Walter, she
was a top-flight computer salesperson in her home
office. Like Walter, she was making a fine salary
and living well in a lovely suburban neighborhood. Unlike Walter, she had no one to share in
life's daily routine. No steady boyfriend. No regular sex life. No one to make omelettes for, walk the
dog with, or curl up beside on a lazy Sunday afternoon. Basically, Lindsay was needy. Lindsay was
attractive. And Lindsay was looking.

But what about Walter? He had everything a
man could want. At least it seemed that way on
the surface. However, ten years of marriage and
three young children takes a bit of the luster off the
Great American Dream. Gone are the long leisurely mornings of making love and dreaming
about the future. The future has arrived and we're
spending more of it installing the new electronic
garage door opener than planning an escape to the
Greek Isles. Not that marriage is devoid of joy or
happiness or sex. But taking care of all life's little
necessities doesn't leave us with much energy to
spare for emotional or sexual fireworks. Certainly
not on a daily basis.

Walter was the classic victim of this reality. Although he was truly happy with his family and
surroundings, he wasn't challenged or stimulated
by his life. And not through any fault or doing of
his wife or kids. When he met Lindsay, he may not
have even realized it, but he was suffering the
symptoms of the proverbial seven-year itch.

Lindsay longed to share in everything Walter
represented. She was drawn to his maturity, responsibility, success, and family values. He was
nothing like the men Lindsay usually dated—

younger men caught in a struggle to reach adulthood. Walter was a pillar of the life Lindsay envi-
sioned for herself. So, she sings the blues over
drinks at a fancy waterfront hotel. They dance to a
mediocre cocktail lounge band. And the next thing
you know, they are up in Lindsay's suite, tearing
off one another's laminated convention nametags
and sending their clothes flying.

An hour later, Lindsay (who conveniently forgot
that Walter already had a wife and kids) is lying
on his chest picturing herself in suburban heaven.
Walter is thinking about the time, and what in
God's name he is doing in bed with this sexy
young woman while his hotel room phone is probably ringing and recording a voice-mail message
from his kids saying they love him and miss him
and can't wait for him to come home. So goes the
pleasures of *scratching* the seven-year itch!

Field of Broken Dreams

There is no denying that an affair is a sexual
matter. We wouldn't sleep with a woman if we
didn't feel desire for her. For some men, the seven-
year itch is mainly a yearning to remember what it
feels like to have sex with someone other than
their wives. But for plenty of others, lusting in
their hearts is more than enough. We can fantasize
about the bank teller, the baby-sitter, or the next-
door neighbor. We might picture them while we
make love to you, just as you might picture the
postman, or Clint Eastwood, or the lifeguard at the
pool. Hearts aren't broken nor marriages ruined
over these fantasy infidelities. We aren't about to

act on them. But it's not simple lust that drives most men over the brink anyway.

More often that not, we cheat because we perceive that we are not getting what we want from you or our relationship. And I'm not referring to home-cooked meals or kinky sex. Men's hearts wander when our *dreams* don't seem to be coming true. When we feel that the woman we thought we were sharing our life with has gone on temporary emotional leave, or when intimacy has deteriorated to the point where we make love too infrequently and even then, in total silence. We need to communicate, and not just in bed. Our conversations have to go on long after the lovemaking is over. Otherwise the distance between us can grow so wide that we'll let someone else in to fill the void.

As a rule, cheating has less to do with sex than a host of other pressures in a man's life. The job isn't going well. The mortgage is turned down. The boss is a jerk. The car doesn't run, credit card debt is piling up, and the family dog needs an expensive operation. The babe who wriggles into your husband's life is apt to offer him a compassionate ear first and a warm body second. Not that this is any comfort. Once a man has cheated (and gets caught), his wife is either so hurt or so blinded by rage over the violation of her trust that she doesn't want to think about where the roots of the problem might lie. And who can blame her? If we're pawing our secretaries on a business trip while you're tucking the kids in, why should we expect any sympathy? Basically, we don't. But there is a lesson to be learned from Walter's story: there are ways to sense that trouble is brewing before you have a full-blown relationship crisis on your hands. It's worth trying to prevent an affair because there's a good chance that cheating on you is actually the last thing your man wants to do.

"Hogwash!" you say? "All men cheat. Or at least they want to." Well, that might have been true of your mate *before* he got involved with you. Or even more so, married you. Once men cross that bridge of commitment, though, we change. The vast majority of us become loyal, faithful, and attentive to our relationship. We are in love, and often stay that way for a very long time. It's only when our restlessness or unhappiness grows beyond our control that sex with someone else crosses our minds. But even then, we want to work things out, and we try to at first.

Over time, all sorts of standard life issues may start to get ignored. We tell ourselves that the new car we want is too expensive and we put off buying life insurance for another year. We decide that kids can wait, and so can that ski vacation. The money we saved for it has to go towards a new boiler. You stay at the job you hate. We get passed over for another promotion. And all of these major and minor difficulties pile up like dirty dishes in the sink. Neither of us seems willing to tackle the mess first. We can't clean it up, and we don't want to talk about it. And before we know it, there is an undercurrent of discontent flowing through our relationship and a haze of unhappiness clouding the horizon.

That's where a potentially unfaithful man is when sexual opportunity knocks. Perhaps it takes the form of a sexy young intern, the one your husband hired last summer and you hated the instant you saw her in cutoff jeans and floral bikini top at the company picnic. The truth is he never once dreamed of going to bed with her. Okay, well, that's not exactly the truth. Actually, he may have spent quite a few hours fantasizing about peeling off those cutoff shorts and giving her a deep oil massage over every inch of her 21-year-old body. But that wasn't a real consideration. It was lunchroom bravado. Every guy in the office had the same fantasy.

Sexual curiosity alone would never have inspired your mate to make a pass at young Heather. But there was a period there when you weren't talking to him and a lot of pressure was mounting at home, and Heather heard all about it. She became your spouse's friend and confidante. She seemed to understand the little things that were bothering him. (Okay, she probably thought he should quit his job and start that rock band. But she *listened*.) He never intended to end up showering off his guilt with her in the bathroom of her tiny studio apartment. It just happened. Which does not excuse it.

It's one thing to jaw with the guys over a game of hoops about how badly we'd all like to have one wild evening with Heather. It's another to cross the line, be unfaithful, and then find ourselves spinning a web of lies that could end up unraveling our marriage. Untenable a situation as this may be, our behavior may have been inspired by circumstances that you had never even known about, or imagined. Men's dreams are heady stuff. They start around the age we can throw a ball and actually think we are going to become a big leaguer. Most of us grow a bit more realistic along the way.

We give up on pitching for the Yankees, but start to plan a career as a fireman. In our freshman year of college, some of us actually think Poli Sci 101 is the first stop on a campaign to the presidency. We aspire to make our first million bucks in business. Or fly an F-15. Or star in *Hamlet* at "Shakespeare in the Park." We aim for these goals with some silly notion that they are not totally out of reach. And then reality slowly settles in like a foggy day at the beach. As it turns out, we're not going to head a multinational corporation. We'd settle for a bed and breakfast in Maine. We're not going to co-star with Tom Cruise in his next film, but we'd take a good spot on a soap. We're not going to start that microbrewery in the Northwest. We'd be happy to find a job tending bar in Seattle.

Reality can be a sobering experience, and as we settle down in our personal lives, the dull roar of frustration may become a high-pitched whine. Our brains aren't accepting what our lives are telling us: "This is it. Get used to it."

Our unfaithful computer salesman, Walter, was a quarterback in high school, played a little junior varsity ball in college, and covered football for the school paper. His interest in the sport never dulled. But he got married young and channeled his big-league aspirations into making a lot of money. Since that wasn't something he could do as a cub reporter for the local newspaper, he opted for a much quicker fix and went to work as a salesman. He took the immediate cash. The dreams could come later. But then he had his first child, got several promotions, and put the old dreams on hold indefinitely while he sold computers to make big commissions to support his family.

Now this may sound like a perfectly fine life. But Walter *really* wanted to be a football player. And if that proved impossible, he *really* wanted to become a sports writer. And when he got married and thought about great ways to make a good living, he *really* wanted to work in the front office of a professional team. All of those dreams had passed him by.

Now, Helen knew about Walter's dreams. She had listened to his old football stories a thousand times—and she thought they were about as relevant to their present-day lives as the pages of the high-school yearbook. They had no place in reality. What did was saving for three kids' educations and charting out a retirement plan. Walter, in turn, knew that Helen's viewpoint was sane and sensible. Yet, it struck him as sad and a bit absurd to be thirty-five-years-old and discussing senior citizenship!

Helen did not dash Walter's dreams. And Walter did not hold his wife responsible for his fate. As a matter of fact, he was 99 percent satisfied with how his life had turned out. But Walter lived at least 1 percent of every day in fantasy land—as most men do. From boyhood to middle age and beyond, we are dreamers. We play "air guitar" in our cars on our way to work, convincing ourselves that we could be Eric Clapton jamming to "Layla." We flock to sports fantasy camps to act out moments of glory with retired stars from our distant youth. We are almost chemically dependent on keeping some semblance of our dreams alive. And that's where the "Lindsays" and "Heathers" of the world come in.

The seven-year itch is a warning tremor prior to

a mid-life crisis. Although lots of wives do not recognize it as such until a crisis actually occurs, many young single women do! Example? If a man was to tell his wife that he'd like to try helicopter skiing in Wyoming, she would want to know how he planned to make a living with both legs in casts. Heather, on the other hand, would think that this idea was "totally adventurous" and the sign of a free spirit. Likewise, if a man jokingly told his wife that they should quit their jobs and sail around the world, his wife would ask what kind of future their children could expect to have without high-school diplomas. Heather would volunteer to teach them to do macrame along with the natives of the Galapagos Islands. You get the picture.

In real life, when Walter met Lindsay, he and Helen weren't having problems, per se. The bills were paid. The house was fine. The kids were cute. Nothing was especially wrong in Walter's life. But nothing was unbelievably right, either. Similarly, Helen was not mean spirited, nor without dreams. She just represented all the routines and responsibilities of adulthood, marriage, and raising a family. Lindsay had not yet tasted from this well. Private schools, bank loans, gum disease: none of that was real to her. She still wholeheartedly believed that anyone could do anything he put his mind to—and that was exactly what Walter wanted to hear when he was knocking back gimlets at a computer convention and wondering where his dreams had gone.

So there Lindsay was, an attractive, available young woman making Walter feel like a young man without a care in the world. And there he was, wishing he could be free of his dream-dashing adult responsibilities. In that light, it isn't completely impossible to see how Walter slipped up.

I am not condoning Walter's behavior as a reasonable cure for the suburban blues, but merely pointing out that he wasn't looking to "get laid." His sex life hadn't even been suffering. But emotionally, he was wallowing. Lindsay offered an accommodating ear, and a momentary escape.

Sadly, Helen was the affair's unwitting victim. Had she picked up the signs of Walter's unhappiness, perhaps she could have headed it off at the pass. Perhaps not. Wives can't be licensed analysts, psychics, and detectives rolled into one. But if Walter had communicated more, or Helen had taken his moods as the signs of a deeper problem as they were, Lindsay might have remained in the realm of fantasy.

Irresistible Urges

I could cite dozens of emotional reasons why men's eyes wander and hearts stray. But that doesn't negate the simple fact that despite our best intentions and deep love for you, we sometimes get aroused by other women. A sexy gal with one eye cocked our way can turn our judgment to Jello. Some men, including happily married men, completely lose control of their normal sense of decorum when they get a whiff of an "off-limits" woman who seems to be interested in them. How do men deal with this problem?

Jeff, one of the horniest guys I know, had a rather perverse system for controlling his sometimes uncontrollable urges. Back in his single days, he would shave, shower, and masturbate before every date. His logic was simple. If he took care of his libido ahead of time, he could relax and have a good time with the woman he was dating. He could look her in the eye and conduct a real conversation without that nagging urge to leap over the dinner table and start massaging her breasts. Jeff probably wasn't the first guy to use this method. When the mood is right and a man has never been to bed with you and there's any hint of mutual desire, he can be blinded by lust. You could be spilling classified government secrets over linguini carbonara, and he'd be politely nodding his head but hearing nothing as he undressed you with his eyes.

The point of sharing this sordid little secret is to illustrate how powerfully sexual pressure affects men's ability to make decisions. Masturbation is like releasing a steam valve. Take away that horny edge and we can function as human beings. But if the tension hasn't been released in a while, we're like caged animals. At feeding time.

Maybe there have been too many things going on at home to make love. Or perhaps the sex is fine, but undramatic. We do it a couple of times a week, but without panache. We all recognize that sex can have a way of losing its sexuality. It can become a chore. Or a grownup kiss and makeup session after a fight or disagreement. Perhaps a man's sex life has become so entwined with stresses in his family or personal life that he has trouble separating the two. It's not that he's fallen out of love with his mate. But he may have fallen out of lust.

It can happen, even to a couple with a perfectly fine sex life. And this presents a real problem for men, because we get antsy and troubled and start staring at every attractive female body that walks by, wondering what she would be like. Conditions are ripe for a brush fire, and it only takes one spark to start a conflagration.

That's where the other woman comes in. She has all the advantages and none of the disadvantages. We may meet her at work. We'll probably tell ourselves (and you) that there's nothing more going on than a mutual professional attraction. But we might sense that it could be more. The question is, will we allow it to be?

Sally's live-in boyfriend, Ralph, had all sorts of women friends and women co-workers, most of whom Sally knew by name, if not by face. Since she trusted Ralph implicitly, she didn't feel threatened by his female friends. Except for JoAnne. JoAnne was different. "Trouble," was how Sally put it. And Ralph couldn't completely disagree.

There are some women we joke around with all the time. Our good-natured, bawdy joshing by the coffee machine never suggests that a real sexual situation exists. And then there are women like JoAnne. Guys can tell the difference in a heartbeat. Whether it's chemistry or body language or the not-so-subtle hints laden with sexual innuendo, the idea that something more could go on if we wanted it to gets through to us. Ralph definitely sensed it with JoAnne, but tried to play it down when he was with his girlfriend (which was exactly why Sally suspected something might be going on). It came as no surprise to either of them when, after working late one evening, JoAnne came on to Ralph in the parking lot, suggesting drinks at a nice little place she knew. Ralph, who was perfectly happy in his relationship with Sally, put his foot down. Not rudely. Not by making a big deal that would have embarrassed his co-worker and created friction at the office. He just said no.

Anatomy of an affair

"Just say no." That's how to stay out of trouble—if a man wants to. Ralph did. He knew in his heart that JoAnne had more than drinks on her mind. But he valued his relationship with Sally and did not want a few beers and temptation to put him in a situation that could jeopardize that. But what about men who have doubts about their relationships or are questioning their commitments or are unhappy at home? What are they thinking when the woman in the next cubicle starts to work her wiles on them? Something that reeks of danger, no doubt.

At first, men may call their new female work friend a confidante. "We're just two people sharing a few problems," he may tell himself. Sure, he notices a hint of sexual energy, but most men will pretend that it doesn't exist—for about one drink, that is!

But if a man and that other woman stop in for that drink at the cocktail lounge in the hotel on the pike, even once, then the seeds of trouble are planted. For starters, he and she now have "a place." Someplace familiar. Someplace they both feel they can safely repair to. Until it isn't safe anymore. It's the setting for the excuses he'll give to you ("Just having a drink with a friend, honey").

And it's the spot that he'll use to rendezvous with his paramour-to-be.

If you pay close attention, you may be able to tell when your man has crossed this line. If he's had a drink with a woman he feels attracted to, there's a good chance he'll come home and be exceptionally nice to you. He'll make love to you the way he did when you first met. And if that's the least bit out of the ordinary, be suspicious! If your sexual relations have gone stale of late, this is the time to really sniff out hidden problems.

I'm serious. If your husband comes home from work one night and suddenly starts to act like you're on a second honeymoon, consider the circumstances. Ask yourself if there have been any problems. Have you been fighting a lot? Have the kids kept you up until dawn, seventeen nights in a row? Has your sex life withered or died in the past few months? Sure, the renewed passion could be a sign of his renewed commitment. The roses, dinner out, and fantastic lovemaking could be repeated over and over again—in which case you *should* enjoy it. But if you were experiencing a sexual drought, that fact should not be ignored. You and your mate still need to look at why things were not so great before. You need to talk it through, build on your strengths, and really try not to repeat the behavior that led you into the doldrums in the first place. If the two of you don't have this frank discussion at some point, you'll find yourselves right back in the same trap sooner or later. And then what happens?

The second you let your defenses down, guess who is going to rear her competitive little head again? That's right, the woman from the cubicle down the hall. If he is quarreling with you over the same old things for the umpteenth time and getting that familiar tightening of the gut he gets after every fight, then the romantic interlude of the week before will fade like a dead rose. You can bet that "the woman from work" will look all the more inviting the next time she suggests drinks at that place on the pike.

Perhaps you've noticed that I haven't once mentioned sexual fantasy when referring to this woman. She isn't Heather in the cutoffs whom the whole office lusts after. She is a different woman entirely, one who may inspire little interest from anyone but us (because we know there is something going on). At this point, we are also keeping our libidos in check, probably because we are aware of our growing attraction and scared of letting it get us into trouble.

You see, we still don't want to cheat on you. That's not why we got married in the first place. If we wanted to keep lusting after everything that moved, we would have kept dating. But when we took our vows (or co-signed a lease), our honest intent was to retire our penises from the touring circuit. Sure our heads were still on a swivel, and we might have been guilty of the occasional erection non grata, but our commitment was to you. And it still is. We didn't wake up one morning and decide it was time to cheat. But if the walls of communication are tumbling down, temptation tends to seep in. And the "woman at work" might be the wave that breaks the dam.

The emotional logistics of having an affair are grueling. Unless, of course, we just have a hankering to go out and cheat. That is pretty self-

explanatory. But those of us who go out with the
woman from the office for a fifth or sixth time
without sleeping with her? What are we looking
for? What drives us, and what might stop us?

After rendezvousing at the same hotel bar for all
this time under the pretense of talking shop, there
comes a point where we know something is about
to happen. It's similar to a first date, back when
that was legit. We get that nervous feeling in our
chests and every moment seems fraught with passion. By now, we are convinced that there are real
problems at home. Right or wrong, we assume this
to assuage our guilt for the thoughts we are having. Right or wrong, we'll tell ourselves that you
have driven us away, pushed us out of your life, or
ignored us when we needed you most. We are ra-
tionalizing.

A man probably won't make the first move on
the proverbial other woman. He might be tingling
with sexual excitement, but this is still deeply forbidden territory. As aroused as he may be, he is
also terrified. This one sexual advance has the potential to alter his entire life. So a man won't take
the lead. She will, though, sooner or later. He
might even reject her and appear to end the whole
affair right then and there. But only for a day or
two. Because now the idea has life. If things don't
change drastically on the homefront, she knows
and he knows that they'll both be back at that hotel bar—and the next time his answer won't be no.

What constitutes an affair? In a man's mind, it can
run the gamut from regular sex with the same
woman every Tuesday afternoon for a year (while
his unsuspecting wife chauffeurs their kids around
suburbia), to a kiss. Yes, a kiss! During the five years

he's been married, Ethan has cheated on his wife only once. And he did it with a kiss. When Ethan found himself on the brink, he tested the waters but stopped short of diving in. He took the woman up to the hotel room, made out with her, groped for five minutes, then left. And that was it.

As far as Ethan was concerned, that was cheating. He kissed a woman who was not his wife and he gave real serious thought to making love to her as well. The fact that he didn't have intercourse or even get naked with her made very little difference to him. That one kiss had been the culmination of months of sexual tension with a woman he knew from night school. He didn't need to take it any further to know that he had crossed the line. Ethan felt completely rotten. And might still if this brief flirtation with unfaithfulness had not had a positive aspect. It vividly illustrated how far he and his wife had strayed. And by nearly going to bed with another woman, Ethan had a much-needed revelation: He really wanted to mend things with the woman he loved.

Patching It Up

What if your husband *is* having a full-blown affair? Or what if you suspect your lover is flirting with the notion of going to bed with someone else? Whether the damage is done, or is about to be done, there *are* ways to salvage the relationship.

Kevin and Dana had lived together in Berkeley since they graduated from the university two years ago. Their relationship was strong, yet it lacked commitment. Perhaps it was their youth, but neither of them had a sense of emotional direction

guiding them to any foreseeable goal. And not surprisingly, Kevin was beginning to show signs of
restlessness. He had more and more female
friends, and while Dana couldn't prove that he
was sleeping with any of them, as far as she was
concerned, he might as well have been. By the time
she went back to their Maryland hometown for a
three-week winter holiday, her spirit was a bit restless as well.

Kevin had stayed behind because of work, and
the separation was supposed to be good for the
two of them. Only Dana didn't feel good. She felt
that Kevin didn't even know she was gone. She
also suspected that he might be fooling around
with a woman at the office, whom he steadfastly
refused to introduce to her. And she was hardly in
the mood to gleefully ring in the New Year when
she attended a party thrown by a group of her
Maryland friends.

Most everyone was coupled off, except for a nice
young guy named Bruce, who happened to be an
acquaintance of Kevin's. Dana solved the problem
of being alone in front of the TV when the ball
dropped in Times Square by planting herself by
Bruce's side for the first kiss of the new year. It
was a memorable kiss. So much so, that by night's
end, she and Bruce had become lovers.

Of all the people Dana could have gone to bed
with to get Kevin jealous, Bruce was the perfect
target. There was no way in the world Kevin
wasn't going to find out, yet Dana didn't have to
be the one to tell him. Bruce and Dana saw each
other a few more times over the holiday. Dana said
nary a word to Kevin about her new lover, but
Kevin sensed that something was very wrong. He

called a friend who had been at the party, turned up the guilt pressure, and quickly extracted the news that his girlfriend was having an affair.

Talk about an attention-getter! Kevin went bonkers! He assailed Dana by phone (they actually had one $125 coast-to-coast call). He demanded to know why and how she could do this to him. She quickly learned that Kevin had not been cheating on her. But she also learned that he had considered it. In a way, it was a good thing that their crisis occurred long distance, because it gave them time to think—and rethink—their situation.

Dana pretty much instantly regretted her actions. Bruce was a perfectly nice guy, but she had no long-range romantic interest in him. And Kevin, arguably the one who instigated this problem by not paying enough attention to Dana's need for commitment, had a solid week by himself to eat his guts out wondering what he did wrong. All the while he imagined another man making love to her.

Men do "jealousy" differently than women. You seem to hate it when we stare at a shapely woman in a bikini, yet we could care less if you ogle a body-builder type in a tank top and bicycle shorts. (He doesn't bother us because we think he looks like a lumphead, and in our hearts we know you don't want to sleep with him.) Most men are incredibly light-hearted about their woman's wandering eye. Maybe that is the result of our overinflated egos. The boss is hitting on you? Who cares! He's a fool anyway. Every guy at the health club has his eyes glued to you as you lift weights in that ripped old t-shirt? We love having the best-looking girlfriend in the club. But another man making love to you? Goodnight! We go nuts. We aren't nearly as concerned about all the ramifications of this transgression as you are. Yes our relationship may be in jeopardy and yes we should be asking what went wrong and what can we do to fix it, but more likely than not, all we can think about is the fact that some other jerk is touching you! Arrghhh, that hurts.

So Dana's ploy worked—in the short run. She flew back to Berkeley to a pained and repentant Kevin. He spent more time with her and their sex life improved a hundredfold—although the more inventive Kevin grew, the more worried he became that Dana enjoyed his lovemaking only because it reminded her of Bruce. In addition, almost a year later she still couldn't convince him that she wasn't out looking for new lovers every time he turned his head. Although Dana's affair definitely cured Kevin's wandering eye, it also wreaked havoc on their relationship and may well have done some permanent damage—which is why I don't recommend this as a method for extracting a commitment from your man.

When our hearts are wandering and our whole persona seems to be on the lookout, is there anything you can do to help us alleviate this condition, short of cheating on us for revenge? The answer is absolutely, definitively yes! But it requires patience, understanding, and most of all, trust. You have to believe that we love you, and we are not looking to replace you, nor hurt you.

Communication is half the solution. We want you to talk to us. Badly! This dated and unfair notion that men are strong and they don't cry and they don't want to talk about their problems is a bunch of bollocks. It can be incredibly lonely being a man. Marriage, mortgages, and newborns can be a hefty load of responsibility for a 26-year-old boy, even if his job is going well, and there is money in the bank, and little Johnny is doing fine. Your man may be living in terror that the whole house of cards could come tumbling down at any minute.

Dating was simple compared to the responsibility of commitment. All we had to worry about when we were single was getting drunk, getting sex, and watching sports. But there is no training course for marriage. We suddenly take on this whole slew of new obligations and we're supposed to accept them, solve them, or at least cope with them. That doesn't even allow for looking down the road to where we might be in a dozen years. We've always told time by the weekend. Either we had a date, or there was something to do with the guys. The idea that our calendar is now booked up solid for, say, the next sixty years—that is pretty terrifying.

Even though we want you to let us be men in the old-fashioned holding-doors-open-for-you mode, we still need you to take on this life commitment equally with us. It has nothing to do with salary, or job status, or who stays home with the children. This is all about the intangibles: the pressures that weigh on our family structure and the future we are molding. We don't want to go it alone. That doesn't mean you have to suffer every second of every day and then retire to a dark neighborhood pub and cry into your beer over rising interest rates. *We* want to do that. But we do want *you* to understand the pressures we face and the changes we go through. We signed on as a team. There is great solace in facing the bad times together, as well as the good. Besides, we are far less likely to turn to distracting, female outside forces for comfort—as long as we are finding it at home.

The Second Honeymoon

You've replaced every item of underwear with ten pages of the *Victoria's Secret* catalog. The bookshelf is stocked with x-rated videos and sex manuals. You've been doing your Kegel exercises religiously for three months. And still, he's out walking the dog with the next-door neighbor's college-aged daughter, discussing the finer points of Philosophy 101. Are you fighting a losing battle? Not necessarily. If we are honest enough to admit that we enjoy chatting with an attractive junior from Yale, then we're not surreptitiously planning to seduce her out by the high-school tennis courts. We're probably just taking a stroll down memory lane.

One of those memories might be sex in a single bed in a stuffy dormer, but we're also longing for the days of our youth. Tailgate parties, all-night study sessions, following "The Dead" on their New England tour ... we don't get to do that stuff any more. She does! And listening to her tales of passionate youth fills a void. Our stories are dusty old relics that tend to leave a dull ache like a slight hangover, whereas she is a bright window on a world we've left behind. So how are you supposed to compete with that? Well, the answer is, you're not. If you cut us a little slack in the flirtation department, we will be infinitely more tolerable in the long run.

The college reunion is a perfect example. We drag you to our tenth, and while you stand there like a wallflower politely smiling at some dork in madras, we are engaged in a convivial, laughing conversation with an attractive woman who looks just a little too overconfident to be as happy as she says she is. Why do any of us go to these tedious affairs? From a man's point of view, mainly to see a couple of old friends, and figure out which girls got better with age, and which ones grew dowdy and not so special. Back in the college days, these were the women who taught us the meaning of rejection. If we weren't fetching them beers at a frat party, we were watching the back end of their ponytail bouncing off with a guy who wasn't us! Now, it gives us a nice sense of satisfaction to see that the women who wouldn't give us the time of day have become uniformly normal. Not even half as pretty as you are! So, after we've walked around the campus and the reunion weekend is over and we're driving back to the city, we are instilled with a sense of how wisely we have chosen you as our mate. When it comes to our ego, a little flirtation with the inaccessible actually boosts a man's confidence in you. It reminds him that his heart was not wrong. But occasionally, the rest of his body needs a jump start.

Take Ed and Lauren, who met in a sailing class in Connecticut. They dated for a magical, romantic year, and were wed on a cruise around Manhattan on a moon-bathed night the following fall. A picture-perfect romance through and through. The next few years though seemed to be filled with one small catastrophe after another. Jobs were lost, cars were wrecked, back taxes ate up their savings, and in general, they seemed caught on a treadmill that never allowed them even one carefree weekend. Not surprisingly, their romance faded and their sex life dwindled.

Ed, a computer programmer, was out of work after a large corporate layoff. His mood was as low as Lauren had ever seen it. Lauren knew how bad things were when his job-hunting started grinding to a halt every afternoon in time for "Sesame Street," which he would watch as he relaxed with a cold quart of beer. The more listless Ed grew, the harder it became for Lauren to kindle any kind of romance. He wasn't interested in sex, he wasn't interested in comfort. Their relationship was bottoming out in a big way, not through any fault of their own, but thanks to a stagnant economy and an unforgiving string of bad luck. Lauren decided their marriage needed a serious jolt before they both wallowed beyond the point of no return.

She returned home from work on a Friday to find Ed in his usual torpor, having a heart-to-heart with Big Bird on PBS. She took him by the hand, dragged him out of the depression he had worn in the couch, and shuffled him off to the mall. Without knowing what she had in mind, Ed numbly followed. They shopped. For new swimwear, and sailing clothes, and all the paraphernalia needed for a cruise. Still she would not tell him where they were going. The next morning Lauren packed all their suitcases and dragged a bewildered Ed out of bed. A limousine drove them to the airport and in a few hours they were dockside in St. Maarten provisioning a thirty-five-foot sailboat for their own charter. No skipper. Just the two of them, setting off on a sail reminiscent of the early days of their courtship. Granted, they could not afford the trip, and Lauren had to max out three credit cards. But the relationship was in dire straits, and Lauren, a headstrong woman to begin with, had no intentions of watching her life's love wither and die just because of a lousy run of luck.

How difficult is it to imagine what a week of sailing in the Caribbean can do for a marriage? The weather turned their way, breezy and mild. The boat was provisioned like a four-star restaurant, and they set off with Lauren as navigator, skipper, seductress, and cook. That night, they moored in an isolated sandy cove. Lauren prepared a meal fit for royalty and pulled out a bottle of the first good wine they had shared on a date (a vintage Margaux). They dined and drank and danced and made love above deck in the moonlight to the gentle rocking of the boat and a blanket of stars overhead. And that was just the first night. Ed's flagging morale took the jump start, and like the phoenix, their romance rose from the ashes of his depression and their formerly dead sex life. The black cloud that seemed to have been following them was swept away by a week of intense lovemaking in every conceivable port of call.

Ed could have gone out and had an affair. Lauren could have ignored all the warning signs and watched their marriage die. But she had a keen sense of what was wrong and a creative solution to keep the romance alive. Men wander away when they're floundering or hurt in other areas of their lives, sometimes, and you don't seem to notice or care. If you're not there, another woman might look like the answer to our problems. But *you* are who we really want. In fact, the comfort and familiarity of our relationship is the greatest currency we have. No man truly in love with his partner is going to trade that in for a meaningless fling with a stranger. The risk of losing everything for a passing fancy or a stray thrill is far too great, and the payoff infinitesimally small.

CHAPTER 8:

Keeping It Sexy

*H*aving carefully analyzed the innermost workings of the male psyche, there is one confession we have to make. And this will probably come as no surprise to you, but it's true. Sex with the same partner can get boring. After you've done it a couple of thousand times in every conceivable position in every room in the house, it just might lose some of its glow. You know the old joke. If you put a jelly bean in a jar every time you make love *before* you get married and remove one every time you make love *after* you're married, you're going to be stuck with a jar full of stale jelly beans! Men fear that they'll lose interest. And you'll lose interest. And start fantasizing about other men . . . Be honest. We're not the only ones whose minds wander during lovemaking. You've probably fantasized about someone other than your mate once or twice. That handsome new intern at work, for instance. Or Peter Jennings. Or your next-door neighbor. You don't necessarily plan to live out your fantasy. But picturing a new face and body just for a moment can certainly spice up a bland

old routine. So can some racy new techniques—
although every alternative isn't right for everyone.
Please keep that in mind as you read on. Try whatever seems realistic and suitable to your thinking.
You need only subscribe to the games that work
comfortably for you and your mate.

Losing It

After you and your partner have lived together
or been married for a long while, you'll probably
go through a sexual slow-down phase. Most couples do. Maybe you've already noticed a distinct
difference between the man who devoted six
months and half of his life savings to getting you
into bed for the first time two years ago, and the
guy snoring on your couch with the remote control
balanced on his beer belly while you read this and
weep. What happened to the fellow who chased
you, drooled over you, and never seemed to get
enough? He went through a change. Men generally
do, and discovering that our once-raging libidos
are suddenly out on sick leave is at least as frightening to us as it is to you.

You don't have to conduct a door-to-door survey
to see who is having a vibrant sex life and who is
going through the sexual blahs. Just look around
you. Go to Sunday brunch at any cafe or diner
around midday. This is a superb venue for people-
watching. Look at couples' faces. Observe their
hands and feet. The ones who have been sleeping
together for less than six months are still conducting a virtual symphony in body language. Hands
and fingers clutch and curl as if they are still engaged in foreplay. Knees and ankles touch. Feet

find their way into partners' laps, with the most amusing (and distracting) results.

Now, drag your attention away from the scintillating *pas de deux* going on at the next table and take a gander at a few other couples—the ones who have been together for a long time. They're easy to spot. They keep their hands and legs and all other body parts to themselves. They stare at the menu as if it were the original Ten Commandments and diligently concentrate on the breakfast specials as if they were going to unearth something other than eggs Benedict or Belgian waffles.

However, the most telltale signs of the sexually sedate are the eyes. Men's eyes especially. They're not gazing dreamily into their lovers'. They're too busy casing the joint like a fed on a stakeout and focusing in on the couples they think "did it" right before they left for brunch. You know, the ones who don't look old enough to be drinking their Bloody Marys. The ones with that fresh-faced just-got-laid look: raised eyebrows and a goofy grin that refuses to go away. We can practically hear their whispered promises to return to their tiny un-air-conditioned loft as soon as they wolf down a little nourishment and put their sexual refueling to use by doing it four more times with the energy of a sprinter and the creativity of the Pilobolus dance troupe! Boy, do we dislike these couples. We dislike them because we used to be them, and we can't figure out where all our sexual exuberance went.

Why does the male sexual fire go out? Is it something you've done? Or something you haven't? A change in your looks, your body, or your attitude? Maybe it isn't *your* problem at all, but ours—and

ESPN's for providing us with a twenty-four-hour
sports distraction. If you asked a thousand guys
about this, you would get a thousand answers.

Sexual desire for a steady mate seems to wane,
some say, because the chase is more exciting than
the catch. When we were dating, the answer to
sexual ennui was to find a new body. The intercourse might be the same, but the breasts were a
different shape, the legs longer, the butt firmer, and
the whole experience a journey into the unknown.
You see, it wasn't really the package we were so
intrigued with, but rather, the opening of it.

Before we ever laid a finger on your naked skin,
every sexually charged second we spent with you
was an unfinished mystery novel, enticing us to
keep turning the pages. You wouldn't believe the
things we thought about before we slept with you.
What color are you nipples? Does nibbling your
ear make you quiver? Are you a screamer? These
were important, stimulating, earth-shattering issues to us, and we would have waged war to find
the answers.

When the elusive moment finally arrived and
we went to bed together for the very first time,
though—voila—the mysteries were solved. Your
nipples are small and pink. Kissing your neck gets
a stronger reaction than nibbling your ear. And
screamer or no, you vocalized some modicum of
pleasure, or at least surprise. So now we knew, but
there was still plenty to discover.

For the next six months or so, we experimented
with every sexual technique we had the nerve to
initiate. That was fun. Interesting. Good for our relationship. But not possible to continue indefi-

nitely. The pressure to come up with something new every night started to get to us, so we started to gravitate to the lovemaking techniques that were the most comfortable and familiar for us. And even if they involved hanging from the rafters, or bondage on the back of a Harley Davidson, we eventually got a little *too* comfortable and familiar with them. Maybe even a bit bored. Anything anyone does repeatedly is bound to become routine, automatic, and a good deal less enticing then when it was brand new.

This doesn't mean that lovers should break up as soon as they make love the same way more than twice in a row. Or that sex can't be satisfying unless it is different every time. But too much of the same thing can make sex feel like a chore. And once it does, you'll know your sex life is about to take a turn for the worse. To put it bluntly, intercourse for a man can be just intercourse. Insertion. Move around. Feel good. Ejaculate. Nothing wrong with that. But it's not unique—or much of an impetus to keep coming back for more.

Another reason our sexual desire begins to dwindle is because we do something you have been asking us to do for a long time. We grow up and stop thinking about sex twenty-four hours a day! "Odd," you say as your guy decides he has to revise the household budget or repair an appliance before coming to bed. "He didn't have a care in the world when I met him. Why is he suddenly so worried about the broken agitator in the washing machine?" Well, the fact is, we worried about washing machines then too, but didn't tell you. When we were first going out, we believed that the last thing you wanted to hear about was what worried us on a daily basis. That's not sexy or fun. After a wonderful dinner, a great movie, and monumental lovemaking at your place, did you really want to know that our entire division might get laid off on Monday? Or that our car was about to be repossessed? Or that our doctor wanted us to try Prozac? We thought not. And we had no interest in talking about these subjects on our early dates anyway.

Once we are in a relationship, though, our real problems become one of the threads running through our day-to-day lives. And they affect our sexual desire. Given the choice between paying bills or engaging in several hours of vociferous foreplay, of course the bills would never get paid. But we don't always have the choice. It's especially tough to ignore those collection notices. So we beg your indulgence. You don't want a man to make love to you if his brain is in the checkbook. And we don't want to fake it. That's not the stuff enduring relationships are made of.

Along with boredom, bills, and unannounced visits from mothers-in-law, children rank high on the list of factors that can take the snap right out of our sex lives. "Moose" and Sheri know this all too well. They have two little boys, aged five and two. The five-year-old, who is already built like a middle linebacker, has developed an active curiosity about anything that goes on behind closed doors. Short of steel bars, nothing seems likely to keep him in his bedroom through the night, especially if he senses that there's something worth investigating elsewhere. What's more, his two-year-old brother has severe allergies to almost everything in the house, the fridge, and the backyard, which causes near constant worry for his beleaguered parents.

On those rare occasions when Moose and Sheri are in amorous moods at the same time and the house seems quiet enough to make an attempt at what they vaguely recall as lovemaking, one of two things happen. Either their younger son makes contact with a milk product, a moldy waste can, or the neighbor's cat and starts wheezing uncontrollably. Or, the linebacker senses an unnatural silence in the house and bursts in on his parents just as things start getting steamy. Sheri and Moose's sex life wasn't just suffering. It was on the verge of death. Fortunately, they found a relatively simple solution to distractus interruptus.

You know all those nationally advertised hotel "getaway plans"? The ones that show happy young couples jumping into swimming pools and sipping daiquiris or dining on flambé dishes served by a corps of waiters in red jackets? Those hotels aren't catering to out-of-state travelers with an odd compulsion to spend the weekend at an Airport Marriott. No, those rooms are occupied by suburban parents like Moose and Sheri who have been given an overnight reprieve by a kind-hearted relative or baby-sitter. This is a rare opportunity for tranquil dining, leisurely lovemaking, and best of all, a good night's sleep. They don't have to wake up to "Barney"! Yet, they're close enough to get home in a flash if Ginny Sue fills the dishwasher with India ink, or Jimbo uses the family dog for a science experiment, or there's a medical emergency.

I could probably come up with a dozen more reasons why men lose their sexual enthusiasm

from time to time—and every one would be valid.
Yet, the next time your mate manifests symptoms
of ennui, the first question that comes to your
mind will still be, "Is it me?" That's an understandable worry. Lord knows, if every time *we*
were "in the mood," *you* suddenly leapt out of bed
to throw a load of laundry in, or pay bills, or walk
the dog—we'd get a little paranoid too.

But *is* it you? I'd like to reply "never," but that
would not be completely forthright. If you've put
on seventy-five pounds since we first met (not five,
but seventy-five!) your man may grow a tad
underenthusiastic. Have you stopped wearing
your sexy dresses, permanently retired your lace
underwear, and taken to wrapping your unwashed
hair in a bandanna all weekend? Has your sexual
technique slipped from "Advanced Expert Triple
XXX" to "How to Please a Man and Get it Over
With As Quickly As Possible"? Then perhaps you
have contributed to our malaise. Of course, we're
guilty of some of these "sins" also.

We are hardly perfect specimens ourselves.
Maybe your breasts are not going to remain pert
and joyously upturned forever, but our stomachs
probably won't be washboard flat beyond the age
of thirty. What's more, we don't expect you to re-
live every playful moment of our courtship every
day of the week. We once were both a lot friskier.
You would perform oral sex at the drop of a hat.
We were willing and able to make love five times
in a weekend. Of course, we were younger then.
Age takes its toll in more ways than one.

But just because we don't make love to you as
often doesn't mean we don't find you sexy. It
doesn't mean that we love you any less. And it

doesn't mean that we are sleeping with our secretaries. Not even the cute one you wanted to mangle at the Christmas party for calling you "Mrs. Smith," even though you are only nine months older than she is. The fluctuations in our sexual enthusiasm most likely have nothing do with how attractive we find you.

You drove us wild when we first met. We loved your face, your body, and the way you made us groan. That really hasn't changed. What has is the nature of our relationship. We're not young lovers anymore. Our sex life has to adapt. And we both have to make the effort to keep it alive. If we hang our hopes and hats on the notion that we're going to remain perpetually seventeen and perpetually horny, we are setting up unbelievably false expectations. But if we both realize that a lifelong sexual relationship is vastly different than a one-night stand, then we can find a million and one ways to make sure the sparks keep flying.

The Surprise Element

If you've been sleeping with the same person for a good long time, then you each know every inch of the other's body. Together you've tried every position and technique imaginable. There are not a lot of surprises left. But there are ways to take the knowledge you have and use it to your sexual advantage. You might start with timing. As the old adage goes, it's everything. Or at least it can be.

Mary, a sexy and successful set designer, had made it into her mid-thirties without getting married. It wasn't that she didn't want to be involved. The right men just weren't asking, and the wrong

ones were constantly knocking at her door. But
then her old boyfriend Christopher reappeared.
Mary and Chris had gone out for about ten months
the last time around. The relationship had been
fine. The sex terrific. Unfortunately, when their
high-flying careers took them to opposite sides of
the globe, their affair fell apart.

Five years went by before Mary and Chris happened upon each other at a mutual friend's gallery
opening in Philadelphia. Both still single, and quite
a few years wiser, they started dating again and
quickly fell back into bed. It was nice ... easy ...
comfortable. But maybe because they had both
been down this road before, something seemed to
be missing. There was romance and friendship,
laughter and intimacy. But their sexual spark
hadn't quite reignited. Until Mary caused a bit of
spontaneous combustion, that is.

After a quiet evening at a popular coffeehouse,
she and Chris headed for his apartment, presumably to climb into bed, have satisfying but unspecta-
cular sex, and drift off to sleep, as usual. But on
this particular evening, Mary did the unusual. She
turned on the heat while they were still in the elevator. She kissed and groped and made x-rated
promises all the way to the twelfth floor. When the
elevator doors opened, Chris tried to lead her out
and take her back to his apartment, but Mary
wouldn't budge. She pressed the button marked
"Close Door" and all the ones with numbers—
twenty-four in all. Then, with the door opening
and closing on every floor and only the late hour
to prevent Chris's neighbors from catching them in
various stages of undress, they rode up and down
for almost forty-five minutes—which was more

than enough time for some very heavy petting and one of the best blow jobs Chris had ever had.

What's so great about a blow job in an elevator? Well, everything! But besides that, many men find the risk of discovery incredibly exciting. By initiating foreplay and performing oral sex where and when she did, Mary had already thrown Chris's psyche a curveball. Add to that the chance that one of his neighbors might have walked in on some portion of this event, and she had a very stimulated boyfriend.

Most men are more than a little fond of oral sex. But like anything else, it can become routine. There's nothing routine about being gobbled up in a public place, though. Your hand slipping into a man's pants when he least expects it can arouse the dead. And a change of venue heightens even the most predictable of sexual situations. The standard Saturday night *"après*-pizza-and-video" foreplay takes on epic proportions when you spring it on your guy in the back booth of a four-star restaurant or the powder room at your Aunt Marge's house while your parents' fortieth anniversary party is going on outside the door.

For Ron and Evie, moving into a terrace apartment near the harbor in Seattle juiced up a sex life that Ron used to call "not bad, but not hopping." One night after dining on the terrace and sipping wine as the sun set, Evie, feeling quite playful, started seducing Ron—and undressing them both—in full view of anyone in the vicinity who cared to look. "I wouldn't have picked the terrace myself," Ron says, "but Evie took the initiative." And being something of a voyeur himself, Ron was soon getting a kick out of putting on a show for others. As ferryboats glided along below them and the city lights shimmered above, they made love on the terrace—which took on a whole new aura after that. Ron and Evie never knew what might happen when they were out there—even in the middle of the day—and a raised eyebrow followed by a glance towards the sliding glass doors became a signal, letting one partner know that the other was up for some sort of outdoor sexual adventure.

Whether it's in the presence of potential onlookers or behind locked doors and curtained windows, if you can catch a man off guard the way Mary and Evie did, there's little doubt that his usual desire combined with the thrill of being offered a completely unexpected treat will make good things happen. In fact, confounding his expectations and convincing him that there's no way to predict what you might do next can keep him in a constant state of arousal.

Even if your normal sex life is brilliant, your partner still might like to be surprised occasionally. Such was the case for Jodi and Tom. To hear them talk, if lovemaking was an Olympic event, theirs would win medals for athleticism and artistry. But there was one small problem. Jodi was often "in the mood" in the evening, whereas Tom was very much a morning person. This didn't deter them from making ends meet, but it always took some planning, which at times snuffed out the spontaneity Tom preferred.

Jodi knew how Tom felt about this, because they had talked about it. Like most couples with healthy sex lives, they also had an open channel of communication for discussing their sexual needs, desires, and dilemmas. Although talking didn't always take care of the immediate problem, in this instance, it paved the way for a pretty creative solution. The next time Tom had to sneak out the door at dawn to catch up on some work, Jodi snuck out behind him. She tailed him to his cubicle in a large office, and ten minutes after he logged on to his computer terminal, appeared before him wearing her raincoat and a smile. Nothing more. You can imagine the effect.

The sight of his wife, naked beneath her raincoat, and the knowledge that she had followed him through the city streets that way drove Tom wild. They ravaged each other on the table of a nearby conference room—and would have tried for an instant replay in the reception room if they had not heard the first of Tom's four hundred fellow employees arriving for work. This one rendezvous jazzed Tom up for months to come. Sex in a new place. Sex with the risk of discovery. Sex at his favorite time of the day. Jodi lit a fire under her husband—just as she had intended. And he loved her for it.

Most men would. So, go ahead. Use your imagination to spice things up. Nothing is too outrageous in our minds. Just try us!

Beyond Technique

How do you and your mate make love? Is your boyfriend on top every time? Does intercourse begin with the same foreplay, segue to oral sex, then culminate in the same manner in the same position for virtually the same amount of time, every time, time after time? Wouldn't you like some variety?

We would. One of the reasons men get such a kick out of dirty videos is because we like watching men and women having sex in ways and positions we've rarely, if ever, experienced personally, and in most instances, wouldn't expect of you. Porn stars do some amazing things with their bodies. Or maybe it isn't so amazing, but rather, very different than what we are used to.

If your lover is glued to *Pixies III: Cheerleaders Meet the Hockey Team*, I promise you, it isn't for the plot. It could be that your sex life has taken on such a familiar ring that he is turning to videos for much-needed variety. If you want to keep him out of the "Adults Only" section of the video store, one surefire way to do it is to try a few "Pixies" tricks yourself. As a matter of fact, it might not be the worst thing in the world if you snuck in an hour alone with some of those films. See what all the excitement is about. Or watch a few with your lover. You both might get some new ideas or become willing to try things you never would have considered otherwise. You don't have to become a porn star to please us. But we certainly wouldn't mind if you occasionally offered us newfound pleasures.

Take Joan and Jeffrey, for instance. He was a claims adjuster of the most conservative stripe, whereas Joan was an advertising creative director, and reputedly, a sexual dynamo. Intellectually, the two hit it off fine. But in bed, the insurance profession was living up to its name: boring! When making fun of former lovers, Joan's favorite jab was "He's the kind of guy who only does it with the lights off." Joan, who clearly was a "lights on" person, easily could have left Jeff in the dark, but she had a warm spot in her heart for him and was willing to administer a crash course in the fine art of driving *her* to distraction.

Gleefully getting into her role as sex educator, Joan would drag Jeff by the tie to her loft, force him down on the couch, and very slowly, very methodically undress both of them, making every step along the way a titillating experience. The more Jeff wanted to take charge, the harder she would fight him. If he tried to go down on her, she would only allow him to play with her breasts. If he wanted her to lie on her back, she would wrestle him over and climb on top. When Jeff was ready to explode, she would crawl off of him and start all over again from scratch. In this manner Joan took Jeff, a seemingly hopeless case, and turned him into a model of sexual inventiveness. He benefited. She benefited. And they've managed to stay together for close to six years now.

When you consider sexuality's countless possibilities, there's no reason why two people should exhaust them in less than, say, a dozen years. When you first become lovers, the very fact that you are having sex is turn-on enough. But after a while, men need variations on the theme just to keep in tune. Technique is not limited to how you move your hips. A man wants you to experiment with his body, and he wants to experiment with yours. Does he finish quicker than you'd like? Try shifting your focus to some other part of his body if he seems too excited. You'll make foreplay last for hours. Spend time teasing only your lover's chest. Every inch of it. Just because your breasts may be your man's lifelong obsession does not mean that his are not just as sensitive. (If you've tried this with your lover, then you know what I'm talking about. If you haven't, then go find him immediately, unbutton his shirt, and go to town. You'll have a captive—and very appreciative—audience.)

Balls! What are you supposed to do with them? Hopefully, whatever it is, you'll do it gently. But don't ignore them. Boy, are they sensitive, and boy, are we open to suggestion.

Girls discovered how to make men come way back in high school when you were first learning to unsnap our 501 jeans. We figured out how to make women come sometime in the heyday of the eighties, when junk bonds were hot and your orgasm carried more weight than the Middle East peace talks. Thankfully, today, simply achieving orgasm is not as weighty an issue. But men still like to make you happy, and get off knowing that they're having some success. We want you to tell us what works. We want you to let us know when we're doing something you like. It helps us keep our sex life exciting.

A little dirty talk can go a long way. Men usually find it incredibly sexy. If we're locked in a vigorous "69" and we suddenly hit pay dirt, let us know. Say something x-rated. Howl. Give us a hint that you're on the verge. It drives men wild, and by the way, inspires them to greater heights of performance. Your verbal reinforcement reminds him that he still turns you on, and that's a powerful incentive to not let his technique slip into the doldrums!

The key to keeping us in peak form sexually is breaking with routine, and technique is a perfect place to do that. There are plenty more ways than one to make love. What's more, sometimes some of the things a couple has done in a traditional or rather sedate fashion can be rewritten and polished to provide a brand-new sexual high.

Just ask Lou, a Brooklyn chef, who has been dating Bonnie, a New York personnel executive. Lou was ready to go to bed with her almost ten minutes after he picked her up for their first date, but Bonnie had no intentions of having sexual intercourse with a new man for a long while. Did her reluctance end their affair before it got out of the starting blocks? Hardly. Bonnie resorted to many men's favorite backup method, the "hand job," and took it to heights that Lou had never experienced.

Most men think of a hand job as something women give to keep them happy, or at least relieve their pain, until you decide to go further. Bonnie treated it quite differently. We're talking seduction, foreplay, baby oil, and explicit attention to detail. Bonnie kept Lou satisfied, manually, for almost four months, until she felt comfortable enough to go to bed with him.

For Bonnie and Lou, the hand job was an introduction to lovemaking. For an established couple, it can be a sexy return to your innocent beginnings. Try it in a movie theatre. Or in the car. Or on a crowded beach. It may sound silly and dated and messy to boot, but you might be pushing a button that has not been pushed since your first dates—and those are the buttons that couples interested in livening up their sex lives should always be looking for.

Getting Kinky

When we were horny young adolescents, our bodies were screaming out for action, but you shut us down at the starting gate every time. We were dying to fool around, especially with your breasts—which is why, when you finally let us get to second base, we played with them until your nipples were sore and our thumb and forefingers were numb. What was so blissfully wonderful about those first explorations was the freedom to do what had been forbidden before. It was the quintessential opening of Pandora's box. What had once been held at arm's length was now available for exploration. We were kids in a candy store.

Now we are adults and old lovers. But who's to say that there aren't dozens more Pandora's boxes waiting to be opened? Why should our sense of discovery be unplugged just because we've run through what is considered the traditional gamut of sexual activity?

Think back to the very first time you sat in that old Buick with your first boyfriend. The first time before you had done anything except make out. There you are under the yellow glare of the school parking lot lights. It's getting late, and your parents are going to kill you if you aren't home by midnight. But you really like this guy. You like him enough to let him touch you, which you've never let anyone do before. Not your naked breasts, not down there, nothing. And so you're fooling around with him, and he's fumbling with your bra and feeling you for the first time. Bare skin. Fingers on your nipples. Hands dipping beneath the belt of your jeans. Can any of us ever recapture the vivid electricity of those first moments?

Perhaps we still can, because there are vast areas of sexuality that many of us have not explored. What is kinky? Maybe nothing more than turning the page on everything you have always done in bed, and starting to try out new and exciting ways to make love. Men love the whole idea of kinky. We also like down and dirty, raunchy, perverse, and maybe even a sprinkling of weird. There is a cable station in New York City that runs x-rated ads for bizarre sexual outcall services. Several million New Yorkers have access to this pornographic late-night extravaganza. In most couples, the woman thinks this channel is disgusting, and never watches it. The man waits until she has gone to bed and flips it on so he can get his fix of lesbian sisters, whips and chains, and seething orgies. Granted, some of what he sees could fall under the heading of "truly sick behavior," but a great deal more simply piques his curiosity. You could too.

When I talk about exploring the kinky I'm talking about *mutual gratification*: doing whatever you and your partner can come up with to turn on *both* of you as you've never been turned on before, *without* turning off, violating, or victimizing either of you. Masturbation is one possibility. Watching a woman masturbate happens to be a major male fantasy. So, if your sex life has been lagging of late, you might introduce a bit of exhibitionism. This could be a planned act or a deliberate accident— the kind that occurs when you "forget" to close the door to the adjoining room where your man just happens to be watching "Gilligan's Island" reruns on a big-screen TV. Climb into bed, get in the mood, and do whatever it is you do best for yourself. Do it loudly enough for him to hear. Hands-down guarantee: if your lover peeked into the bedroom and saw you working yourself into a frenzy, he would either be on top of you in a heartbeat, or watching in secret from the doorway and taking his problem into his own hands. This leads to another low-risk, big-payoff option—mutual masturbation. Every couple I know who has admitted to trying it gives it rave reviews. Now this is not sick stuff. Nearly all of us masturbate. Why not share in the fun?

Another area where couples slip into the danger zone of the too familiar is the exploration of each other's bodies. The first time your man saw you nude, chances are, he wanted to give you a tongue bath from head to toe and set up camp in the crook of your arm for about six months. With any luck, you weren't half-displeased with his body either. How is it then, that one day we wake up to find our bodies being used for nothing more than test probes for doctors or fixtures on a Lifecycle seat? When was the last time you really seduced your lover? And encouraged him to really seduce you? Men are just crawling with erogenous zones waiting to be discovered. You can chart a relief map on your boyfriend's body with your fingers and your mouth, or you can go to the fridge and really test the waters.

Get a bottle of nice wine, some ice, some fresh fruit, and something sticky and sweet. (Do not use your best sheets for this exercise.) Gently bind your man to the bed (silk scarves seem to be back in vogue). Strip him down and create a tasty trail across his body with any food item you like. Peanut butter. Strawberries. Chocolate syrup. There must be some place on his body where you would like to lick that off. Encourage him to turn the tables and drizzle Amaretto down your breasts and onto your belly then lick off every sweet drop. This won't harm you and it's virtually guaranteed to arouse him.

The video camera may be one of the great untapped sexual breakthroughs of the twentieth century. Take a breather from home movies of the kids playing on the beach. Find out what kind of thespian you are. Let your partner direct and videotape you putting on a show for him. You don't need the moves of a professional stripper to excite him. Your innocent, slightly embarrassed fumblings are more than enough. If you are shy and nervous about undressing in front of the camera, the result is going to drive a man wild. The sight of you in the spotlight, at first hesitating, then slowly peeling off your clothes, then maybe getting into it and starting to explore yourself can be a wonderfully arousing experience for your lover. And hopefully for you too. And remember, that camera can also shoot him.

There is a whole new cottage industry that has sprung up from couples videotaping their lovemaking and selling the results. You don't have to put your private collection on display, but two lovers with an open mind can uncover a whole new side of their sexuality. Men have been renting x-rated videos since the invention of the VCR. You might be surprised at the level of excitement both you and your significant other feel after starring in your own triple-x film.

What you choose to do to keep the juices flow-

ing in your sex life is only as limited as your sense
of adventure. There is a whole world of unex-
plored treats waiting to be tapped. Nothing you do
has to be morally reprehensible and it absolutely
should not be forced or painful. But as two consenting adults with healthy libidos and imagina-
tions, there is no reason to limit yourselves to the
traditional, the routine, or the sleep inducing.

Getting Really Kinky

Darrell, a struggling actor, and his wife, Erin, a
fellow struggling actress, were home one hot summer's night bemoaning the usual lack of work and
income. They were joined by an acting-class
buddy, Doug, who happened to have recently been
paired with Erin for some heavy love scenes. The
three of them smoked a couple of joints, drank a
couple of beers, and got pretty loose and giddy. So
much so that when Erin and Doug started play-
fully reenacting the love scene, Darrell, instead of
belting his friend, joined in, and the three of them
had what I call a "real life" *Penthouse* experience.

You'd be hard-pressed to find a man who has
not at one time or another read *Penthouse*'s letters.
You know, the presumably true stories that often
begin: "I never dreamt I'd be writing this, but I
was at a party last week with three coeds from a
large midwestern university . . ." The men in these
letters always have nine-inch penises, and the
women are young innocents who, with the help of
a sorority sister, have just discovered the hidden
pleasures of their bodies. Sadly, we doubt that any
of these stories actually happened. But we live in a

constant state of awe, hoping against hope that just once, one of them would happen to us.

In Darrell, Erin, and Doug's case it did. To the best of my knowledge, their "threesome" was a once-only event, but not all that unusual. Based on the stories I've heard, *ménage à trois* involving two men and a woman actually happens more than you'd think. But one thing's for sure. Men find the *idea* of a threesome to be an incredible turn-on. For many, being part of one has been a lifelong sexual dream. Generally, we'd prefer it to be with two women. That is the holy grail of male fantasy— two attractive women making love to each other, then inviting the man to join in. We are vaguely aware that this scenario doesn't have the same appeal for most women. Making love to another woman crosses the boundary into bisexuality, and that is not an easy transition for a dyed-in-the-wool heterosexual female. Being watched may not turn you on either. But that doesn't stop men from dreaming that you'd consider sharing this fantasy, perhaps just once.

Mate-swapping is another really kinky activity that does go on in some circles—although in most it is known as cheating and has a tendency to break up marriages. Two couples playing strip poker with a videocamera one drunken night is the closest anyone I know has come. They didn't get physical with each other, and to the best of my knowledge, their game was not a prelude to further explorations, but they were willing to push the envelope of sexuality just a bit. Just a little risqué game-playing can provide a huge thrill.

I really can't make a serious argument for mate-swapping, threesomes, or letting us watch you make love to someone else in order to fire up your long-term sex life. Wishful thinking aside, most men recognize that those acts are *way* out there in the ionosphere of kinkiness. But they still have a huge store of sexual energy caught up in those and other "forbidden fruit" fantasies. It is the spine-tingling idea of treading on dangerous, uncharted ground that appeals to us—you don't ever have to act on a fantasy, but it can be a mutual turn-on just to contemplate it.

Mental Games

Never underestimate the power of the male libido. We are creatures of fantasy. We undress every woman who walks by. We mentally make love to grocery store clerks, our secretary, and the girl on the rowing machine at the club. Sometimes we do this while we are making love to you. We lie on the beach kneading suntan lotion into your shoulders and think about peeling off the bikinis of the seven college girls sleeping on the next blanket. We apologize. We can't help it. It's in our genes. Your best bet is to tease us, torture us, and drive us wild by becoming part of our fantasies.

There is no use getting angry. If we are gawking, obvious fools, we deserve to have you box our ears on occasion. But you'll rarely catch us. We have developed a personal surveillance system to go with our fantasy life, and you will never uncover it entirely. Any slip-up you might spy is only the tip of the iceberg. We don't mind if you have fantasies. So why not indulge us in ours? And perhaps use them to your advantage.

Tracy did. Like most males, her husband, Peter

was an incorrigible breast man, and she was on to his little game of always positioning himself for the best glimpse of other women's cleavage. He was especially voyeuristic in the summer when so much tanned flesh is on display. It's not that he *needed* to look elsewhere to see great breasts. His wife was more than amply endowed. He simply was a connoisseur who got a thrill from the stolen glimpse.

So how did Tracy get back at him? With a simple little game. One particularly sultry summer afternoon as they were waiting in a long movie line, Peter was behaving true to form and gazing at every skimpily clad woman who walked by. He nearly knocked over an old lady to sneak a peek at a bikini-clad coed on rollerblades. What Peter hadn't noticed was that Tracy was wearing a tank top and no bra under the cotton button-down shirt she had put on to stay warm in the air-conditioned theater. As they sweated outside on the movie line, Tracy peeled off the outer shirt, revealing her firm figure barely covered in the tight tank top. Peter, forever on the prowl, still didn't notice. But about six beefy guys in the movie line did, especially when Tracy made a fine show of bending down to tie her shoelaces and revealed her breasts to every man within twenty yards of her. *Then*, Peter noticed. He was shocked. And totally aroused. In his case, knowing that every man on line was gazing at his wife's breasts turned him on.

Yes, we are jealous by nature. And yes, there was a time when it would kill us to think that other men might even be looking at you. But if we've been together for a significant amount of time, then we haven't had that sick, jealous feeling in the pit of our stomachs for a while. We're definitely going to feel it again if your breasts or any other feature is drawing leers from every goofball in your general vicinity. Mind you, some men do get nasty when you attract gazes from other males— and if you know your guy is one of them, Tracy's little attention grabber probably isn't one you should try. But for most of us, the idea that another man is admiring you makes us sit up, take notice, and lust after you even more.

That's why relationships that break up temporarily sometimes resume with a sexual vengeance after the man learns his ex is fooling around with someone else. This is not an invitation to go out and have an affair, but if you occasionally trot out your sexuality for the rest of the world to see, he'll remember how lucky he is to have you for his own.

Even when a couple's sexual compatibility is at an all-time high, and their bedroom is a den of sex toys and dirty home movies, women can still intensify men's arousal by messing with their minds. A little playful cruelty can go a long way here. If for whatever reason your man has been less than attentive in the sex department, think about holding out on him. Lock the old chastity belt and hide the key! No warnings, though. That ruins all the fun. Just keep him on his side of the bed against his will for a little longer than he is accustomed to. Sure it's a game, but you know a man's sex drive grows logarithmically with each passing hour when he doesn't get any. It's utterly predictable. If we don't have sex for a few days, we are going to start wanting it. That is when your little ploy becomes an effective tool.

Marti is a busy ad executive who travels a great deal on business. Her boyfriend Neil had a bothersome habit of frequenting the neighborhood pub a few nights a week right around Marti's bedtime. He was happy to roll in after a couple of pints and make love, but Marti was tired of having the bulk of her sex life take place in a dream state. So she closed up shop.

At first, Neil didn't notice. But then the old sexual tension started to work its way into his bones. One night he actually passed up a run to the pub and made a play for his girlfriend. Alas, she just "wasn't in the mood."

The next morning Marti was leaving for St. Louis on a three-day business trip, and with Neil watching, made a very big deal of putting on her sexiest lingerie underneath her most provocative suit. The one Neil liked to jump her in, whenever she wore it out with him. On this particular morning, it jolted him out of a near-dead sleep. He asked her point-blank if she was sleeping with her St. Louis client. Marti smiled a smile he had never seen before and didn't really answer.

When she returned home, Marti was greeted by a chastened boyfriend, to say the least. You see, the possibility that his girlfriend might be seeing and sleeping with someone else had been a sobering thought, quite literally. Suddenly his nightcaps at the local bar seemed like a lousy investment of time.

That evening, following a romantic, candlelit dinner for two, Marti led Neil away from the table, lowered the lights, and with Miles Davis playing soulfully in the background, made a slow, sensuous production out of peeling off her sexy suit one button at a time. Apparently, while in St. Louis, Marti had a few spare moments to go shopping, because she had all new sexy lingerie on underneath. The effect was more than a little gratifying for both of them. Marti and Neil made love on the butcher block in a damp bed of arugula! He did not go out to the pub that night. As a matter of fact, he hasn't been out for a nightcap without Marti in six months.

When used *sparingly*, mind games like Marti's can go a long way. The only thing more active than a man's libido is his imagination. Put a few racy thoughts in his head and he'll run with them—right to your side. Add a surprise or two, a little kinky good-natured fun now and then, and just a shadow of a doubt about his exclusive hold on you, and he's hooked.